STUDIES IN EUROPEAN HISTORY

XVI

A HISTORY OF

THE ESTATES

OF

POITOU

by

JOSEPH M. TYRRELL

1968

MOUTON

THE HAGUE · PARIS

LIBRARY OF CONGRESS CATALOG CARD NUMBER: 68-13348

Printed in The Netherlands by Mouton & Co., Printers, The Hague

To My Wife

PREFACE

The purpose of this book is to examine the history of the estates of Poitou from its origins in the thirteenth and fourteenth centuries until its disappearance in the mid-seventeenth century. The author of a study of this sort is always faced with the problem of deciding between a topical and a chronological approach. After some deliberation, I have decided to include a detailed Catalogue of Assemblies in an appendix to provide the necessary chronology and devote most of the book to a topical discussion of the subject.

I am particularly indebted to Professor J. Russell Major of Emory University who directed my doctoral dissertation from which this study is derived. His help and advice, both then and since, have been of inestimable value to me. I am grateful to my colleagues at Old Dominion College, Professor William J. Schellings, who read my entire manuscript and suggested many improvements, and Professor Heinz K. Meier who helped me reorganize the section on financial activities.

I owe a debt of gratitude to several archivists in France for their cooperation, particularly M. François Eygun, archivist of the town of Poitiers, who helped me decipher several almost illegible fifteenth and sixteenth century documents.

My research in France was financed in part by a grant from the French government. To Old Dominion College I am obliged for financial help received at various stages of my work.

The material dealing with the financial activities of the estates of Poitou originally appeared in *Mediaeval Studies*, and it is reprinted in this book with the permission of the editors.

Finally, I am indebted to my wife, not only for her help in typing and proofreading, but for her patient encouragement throughout the long period of research and writing that this book required.

Norfolk, Virginia   JOSEPH M. TYRRELL
December, 1965

TABLE OF CONTENTS

ABBREVIATIONS

A. C. Poitiers	Archives communales de Poitiers
A. D. Vienne	Archives départementales de la Vienne
A. H. P.	*Archives Historiques du Poitou*
A. H. S. A.	*Archives Historiques de la Saintonge et de l'Aunis*
A. N.	Archives Nationales
B. N.	Bibliothèque Nationale
B. S. A. O.	*Bulletin de la Société des Antiquaires de l'Ouest*
M. S. A. O.	*Mémoires de la Société des Antiquaires de l'Ouest*
n.a.	nouvelles acquisitions, manuscrits français, Bibliothèque Nationale
p.o.	Pièces originales, Bibliothèque Nationale
Régistres de Poitiers	Régistres des déliberations de la ville de Poitiers

INTRODUCTION

At Warsaw in 1933 the *Congrès International des Sciences historiques* approved a proposal to set up a commission for the study of the history of assemblies of estates. The aim was to apply the comparative method to a subject hitherto studied for the most part on national lines. It was hoped that international co-operation might substantially advance our understanding of the origin and development of medieval representative institutions. The *Commission internationale pour l'histoire des assemblées d'états* was formally constituted in 1936, and has also been known since 1950 by its second name, the *Commission for the History of Representative and Parliamentary Institutions.*

Since the formation of this Commission, a large number of books and articles have been written in Europe, Canada, and the United States dealing with European representative institutions in the Middle Ages. They have shown such a diversity in the interpretations of the origins and development of these institutions that it is apparent that much detailed research must be done on many of the individual estates before the comparative method can be applied effectively.

In the case of France, much has already been written on the Estates General. It is the opinion of some historians, such as Henri Prentout, that greater value lies in the study of French provincial estates. He believes that they were better adapted to the tendencies of the different regions which made up France, and consequently had more vitality than the Estates General. To study them is to study "that which is permanent in representative institutions in France".[1]

Excellent works have appeared on the estates of some of the larger provinces, such as Normandy, Languedoc, and Brittany, and on those of several of the smaller regions, such as Velay.[2] Of those provinces

---

[1] Henri Prentout, "Les Etats provinciaux en France", *Bulletin of The International Committee of Historical Sciences*, I (Washington, Oct. 1926-July 1928), 633.

[2] Henri Prentout, *Les Etats provinciaux de Normandie*, in *Mémoires de l'Aca-*

whose estates have not yet been studied, one of the largest and most important is Poitou. Thomas, in the introduction to his excellent work on the provincial estates of central France,[3] stated that he planned to extend his study to Poitou and Saintonge. He never carried out this project, and nothing has yet been written on the estates of either province.

One point that should be made clear at the outset is the distinction between *pays d'état* and *pays d'élection*. During the sixteenth, seventeenth, and eighteenth centuries, it was customary to divide the provinces of France into these two categories. In the former, the provincial estates survived and approved royal taxes. In the *pays d'élection* the provincial estates no longer met regularly and taxes were imposed and apportioned directly by royal officials known as *élus*. From the mid-fourteenth until at least the mid-fifteenth century, however, the distinction between *pays d'état* and *pays d'élection* is not valid, and virtually every *pays* of France had active estates. Although this fact has been pointed out by several writers, notably Dupont-Ferrier,[4] it seems to have escaped some historians. Moreover, even in the sixteenth and seventeenth centuries when, in many provinces, the estates no longer met regularly and no longer voted royal taxes, they were still assembled occasionally for certain purposes. This will be demonstrated in the case of Poitou.

As far as terminology is concerned, historians disagree about the proper use of the terms "provincial" estates, "particular" estates, "estates of a *baillage*", etc. The distinction seems to be somewhat academic. In this work, the three orders meeting together will be described as the three estates of Poitou, or simply the estates of Poitou.[5] More restricted

---

démie Nationale de Sciences, Arts, et Belles-Lettres de Caen, Nouvelle Série (Caen, 1925), 2 vols. Henri Gilles, *Les Etats de Languedoc au XVe siècle*, in *Bibliothèque Méridionale*, Second Series, no. 40 (Toulouse, 1965). A. Rébillon, *Les Etats de Bretagne de 1661 à 1789* (Paris and Rennes, 1932) hereafter cited as Rébillon, *Les Etats de Bretagne*. E. Delcambre, *Les Etats du Velay des origines à 1642* (Saint-Etienne, 1938), hereafter cited as Delcambre, *Les Etats du Velay*.

[3] Antoine Thomas, *Les Etats provinciaux de la France centrale sous Charles VII* (Paris, 1879), hereafter cited as Thomas, *Les Etats provinciaux*.

[4] G. Dupont-Ferrier, "De quelques problèmes historiques relatifs aux états provinciaux", *Journal des Savants* (Aug.-Oct., 1928), pp. 353-57; hereafter cited as Dupont-Ferrier, "De quelques problèmes", *Journal des Savants* (Aug.-Oct., 1928). See also P. Ninglat, "Des états provinciaux sous le règne de Louis XIV", *Revue des Sociétés Savantes des Départements*, ser. 2, II (1859), 60.

[5] The use of these two terms interchangeably is merely a matter of convenience and is not intended as an endorsement of the somewhat outmoded theory that all three orders must be meeting together before the term "estates" can be used.

assemblies will be described according to their composition; for example, an assembly of the nobles of Poitou.

A detailed narrative history of the estates of Poitou is not possible owing to the lack of any minutes of their meetings (*procès-verbaux*) prior to 1559. Nevertheless, it is possible to piece together numerous fragments of information and obtain a fairly clear picture of their role and nature. Most of the remainder of this book, then, will be devoted to a study of the functions, activities, organization, and procedure of the three estates of Poitou.[6] First, however, it is of interest to examine briefly their frequency of meeting.

As might be expected, the activity and importance of the estates of Poitou were by no means constant throughout the long period of more than two and a half centuries from the time when it first began to meet frequently in about 1390 until its disappearance in 1651. Indeed, the institution underwent some very fundamental changes. Although the changes were gradual, the history of the estates of Poitou between these years can be divided into four fairly distinct periods.

The first period was from about 1390 to about 1435 when the chief function of the estates of Poitou was to vote taxes. Between these years there were thirty-two definite meetings and five probable meetings of the three estates. In addition, there was one assembly of the clergy and one assembly of the barons. Although documents are somewhat rare before 1411, they are sufficient to indicate that the estates met frequently between 1390 and 1411. From 1411 to 1435, they met almost every year, and sometimes two or three times within a year. In about 1435, the estates of Poitou ceased to consent to royal taxes. This marked an important turning point in its history.

The second stage was from about 1435 to about 1470 when the three estates of Poitou no longer voted royal taxes but still met frequently for a variety of other reasons. Even within this relatively brief period of about thirty-five years, their frequency of meeting was by no means constant. Between 1437 and 1444, they met only once, and this was during the crisis of the Praguerie. They then went through a period of revived activity, meeting eleven times between 1445 and 1454, frequently at the instigation of the town council of Poitiers. During the last seven years of the reign of Charles VII, there is nothing to indicate that they met at all. They were briefly revived in the early years of the reign of Louis XI, meeting seven times between 1461 and 1470. This

---

[6] For a brief description of each meeting, see Appendix A, Catalogue of Assemblies.

latter date marks something of a turning point in the history of the three estates of Poitou as it ended the years of their greatest activity.

The third period, from about 1470 to 1559, might be described as one of occasional meetings for a few specific purposes. The fact that in many provinces of France the estates did not continue to meet regularly after the middle of the fifteenth century did not mean that these institutions were completely dead. "Legally", as one historian puts it, they continued to exist and could be reassembled by the king at any time.[7] The edict of July 1628 which suspended the estates to Dauphiné, acknowledged this by stating that this body could be assembled, with special royal permission, for matters of importance to the king and province, "just as is the case in all the provinces of our kingdom." [8] This shows that even those provinces whose estates were apparently moribund could, with special permission from the king, obtain temporary representation to regulate their relations with the monarch with regard to a specific point. This accounts for the occasional meetings of the three estates of Poitou between 1470 and 1559.

The final period in the history of the three estates of Poitou was from 1560 to 1651. The year 1559 does not mark a fundamental turning point. The king might still have summoned the estates of Poitou at any time that he chose and for any purpose, just as during the previous period. As it happened, however, the only purpose for which it seems to have been convoked after 1559 was to elect deputies and prepare lists of grievances for assemblies of the Estates General. It is for this reason that these years might be considered a separate period in its history. It met for this purpose on seven occasions between the years 1560 and 1651. As nearly as can be determined, the assembly of July 3, 1651, was the last meeting of the three estates of Poitou until the abortive attempt to revive provincial estates in 1787 on the eve of the French Revolution.[9]

The above brief sketch indicates the rather uneven activity of the estates of Poitou during the years of its existence. Before turning to a detailed study of the role and nature of this institution it is necessary to examine its origins.

---

[7] F. Olivier-Martin, *Histoire du droit français, des origines à la Révolution* (Paris, 1951), pp. 399-400, hereafter cited as Olivier-Martin, *Histoire du droit français.*
[8] *Ibid.*, p. 400.
[9] One, and possibly several assemblies of the nobles of Poitou were held during the years 1652-54. These were without royal approval and Louis XIV took steps to prevent them. See B. N., ms. fr. 4184, fols. 366-376, and 4189, fol. 257.

I

ORIGINS

Historians have proposed a number of theories to explain the origins of provincial estates.[1] Of these, the two that seem to merit the most serious consideration as possible explanations of the origins of the estates of Poitou are the feudal council theory and the corporatist theory.

According to the first of these two theories, provincial estates developed from the feudal council and from the duty of a vassal to provide his lord with aid and advice (*auxilium et consilium*). This development was from the feudal council in its plenary rather than its restricted sense. In other words, the estates did not develop from the limited group of vassals who actually attended the lord's court from time to time, but rather from the entire body of his vassals who were obliged to attend if he should summon them. Variations of this theory were set forth by Rébillon, Girard, Luchaire, Molinier, and others.[2] Rébillon and Girard found this theory to be satisfactory in explaining the origins of the estates of Brittany and the Comté Venaissin respectively. Luchaire, while setting forth the same theory, limited it to the Estates General and believed that provincial estates were formed in imitation of this body. This latter opinion is not tenable in the opinion of the present writer. The Estates General and provincial estates seem rather to have been parallel institutions.

The supporters of the corporatist theory hold that, previous to meetings of the three orders, there existed individual social corps or *Standen*.[3] These corporative groups sprang into being spontaneously, in-

[1] For summaries of these theories see Delcambre, *Les Etats du Velay*, pp. 449-53, Roger Doucet; *Les Institutions de la France au XVIe siècle* (Paris, 1948), pp. 337-39, hereafter cited as Doucet; and Dupont-Ferrier, "De quelques problèmes", *Journal des Savants* (Aug.-Oct. 1928), pp. 315-17.

[2] Rébillon, *Les Etats de Bretagne*, pp. 17-21. Joseph Girard, *Les Etats du Comté Venaissin depuis leurs origines jusqu'à la fin du XVIe siècle* (Paris, 1908), pp. 52-53. Achille Luchaire, *Manuel des institutions françaises* (Paris, 1892), p. 255. A. Molinier, "Etats provinciaux", *La Grande Encyclopédie*, XVI, 523-27.

[3] For this theory, see the various writings of Emile Lousse, notably *La Société*

dependent of the territorial power to which at first they were a rival. Gradually the territorial power succeeded in subordinating them to its control, and they became an instrument of government. The monarchical state replaced the corporative state and assemblies of estates appeared, convoked by the territorial power to vote taxes.

It should be noted that the feudal council theory and the corporatist theory are not entirely mutually exclusive. Two of the leading historians of the corporatist school, Olivier-Martin and Lousse, see assemblies of estates developing from the feudal council.[4] However, to them, this is merely a fairly late stage in the development, and they emphasize earlier and deeper social and economic factors that had given birth to the three orders. The chief difference between the two theories is one of emphasis. After a careful examination of the preliminary stages and early development of the estates of Poitou, an attempt will be made to see which, if either, of these theories explains its origin.

In his valuable study of the administration of the apanage of John, duke of Berry, René Lacour states, without adequate proof, that the estates of Poitou seems to have been created by the duke of Berry after the province was recaptured from the English in 1372.[5] Moreover, he believes that it was modelled on the estates of the other two provinces of the duke's apanage, Berry and Auvergne. His explanation of the origins of the estates of Poitou is an over-simplification, although he is probably correct in believing that the three orders in Poitou met together for the first time during the 1370's after the reestablishment of French control.

It was while Poitou formed part of the apanage of John, duke of Berry, that the three estates began to meet regularly for the first time. It is quite likely that the duke's personal role in this stage of their development was of some importance, and it would not be surprising if he were influenced by the previously existing estates of Berry and Auvergne. Nevertheless, the duke cannot be credited with introducing a completely new and alien institution into Poitou. Provincial estates developed gradually in France, and the normal preliminary stages in this development

---

de l'Ancien Régime, I, Etudes présentées à la commission internationale pour l'histoire des assemblées d'Etats, VI (Louvain and Bruges, 1943), hereafter cited as Etudes, and "Assemblées d'Etats", Ibid., VII.

4 Olivier-Martin, Histoire du droit français, pp. 393-94, and E. Lousse, "Assemblées d'Etats", VII, 242.

5 René Lacour, Le Gouvernement de l'apanage de Jean, Duc de Berry, 1360-1416 (Paris, 1934), p. 375, hereafter cited as Lacour, Le Gouvernement de Jean, Duc de Berry.

can be seen clearly in Poitou in the thirteenth and early fourteenth centuries. The process was not completed quite as early in Poitou as in some other regions, such as Auvergne and Berry, but the indications are that it was developing along similar lines and that the action of John, duke of Berry, served at most to hasten this development. For a better understanding of the development of assemblies of estates in Poitou, it is necessary to examine the preliminary stages, paying special attention to the matter of consent to taxation, which was to be the principal activity of such bodies.

Medieval institutions tended to develop in a somewhat haphazard manner, with convenience rather than theory as a guiding principle. As they developed, they became somewhat more clearly defined. It is a mistake, however, to look for rigidity in their early stages.

The above generalizations apply to the development of assemblies of estates. At first there was no fundamental difference in nature and attributes between assemblies of the Estates General of all or part of France, of the three estates of a single province, or even assemblies of one estate of one or more provinces. If, for example, the king or a great lord, sought the consent of the feudal body to what Callery terms an extra-feudal measure, such as an extra-feudal tax, he was under no obligation to assemble the entire feudal body in one place at one time.[6] He could replace the consent of the Estates General by the consent of either assemblies of the various estates of the realm meeting separately, or by assemblies of provincial estates. Consent by provincial estates could be replaced by the consent of the separate estates of the province, or even by the consent of the individuals or representatives of corporate bodies that composed them. The consent of the members of the feudal body to a measure had exactly the same effect, no matter what type of assembly it was given in. The only difference was the numbers involved, and hence the extent of the area where the decision taken could be executed. The king or great lord chose whichever of the above alternatives suited him best under the circumstances.

When consent to taxation was desired, the general policy in the late thirteenth and early fourteenth centuries was to negotiate directly with the individual towns. The nobles and clergy were consulted either individually or in regional assemblies. In the first half of the fourteenth century, the kings frequently summoned large preliminary assemblies

[6] Alphonse Callery, *Histoire de l'origine, des pouvoirs, et des attributions des Etats Généraux et provinciaux depuis la féodalité jusqu'aux Etats de 1355* (Brussels, 1881), pp. 51-53.

of towns or nobles, or sometimes the Estates General. The purpose was probably to explain the king's point of view, or at most to secure the general assent to the necessity of a tax. Negotiations on the local level were still required and in no way replaced.[7]

In the light of the above, it is clear that, in studying the origins of either Estates General or provincial estates, it is necessary to study also these smaller or more limited assemblies which were an alternative and served exactly the same purpose. Such smaller assemblies were at first more common, but gradually the king (or sometimes the great lord in the case of provincial estates) found it more convenient to assemble all three orders at the same place at the same time. In this study, we are concerned with this development on the provincial level. Assemblies of the different orders meeting separately in Poitou in the thirteenth and fourteenth centuries must therefore be examined. Such assemblies appear to have been a preliminary stage in the development of the three estates of Poitou.

There is no record of any assemblies of the clergy of Poitou during the thirteenth and fourteenth centuries for anything other than matters of local church business. According to Canon 6 of the Lateran Council of 1215, annual synods were to be held in each diocese to discuss the affairs of the diocese. This practice seems to have been followed fairly consistently in France in the thirteenth and fourteenth centuries.[8] Presumably, then, regular synods of the clergy of the three dioceses composing Poitou were held to discuss matters of local ecclesiastical business, and these synods probably provided the framework for later assemblies of the clergy of the province.

The first assembly of the clergy of all the dioceses of Poitou of which we have definite knowledge took place in the early part of the year 1402. The bishops of Poitiers, Maillezais, and Luçon and the abbots and other clergy of Poitou assembled in the town of Saint-Maixent and granted an *aide* to the king to be used for the war.[9] This was to be paid "in the customary sum and manner" by the clergy of Poitou for a three year period, beginning the previous October 1, (1401). The document states that the prelates of the kingdom, assembled at Paris, had already agreed to grant an *aide* to the king for the same three year period. The phrase

[7] See Charles H. Taylor in Joseph R. Strayer and Charles H. Taylor, *Studies in Early French Taxation* (Cambridge, Mass., 1939), p. 163 ff.

[8] Paul Viollet, *Droit publique: histoire des institutions politiques et administratives de la France* (Paris, 1890-1903), II, 356, hereafter cited as Viollet.

[9] B. N., ms. fr. 20,886, fos. 108, 109, 110.

"in the customary sum and manner" seems to indicate that earlier assemblies of the clergy of Poitou had met to vote royal taxes.

There is more evidence concerning the assemblies of the nobles of Poitou. During the long period when the region formed part of the apanage of Alphonse de Poitiers (1241-1271) several such assemblies took place. For example, in November 1246 the nobles of Poitou met and named a commission of four high barons to defend their rights against the clergy. They were concerned with ecclesiastical courts infringing on the rights of seigneurial courts.[10] This assembly is of interest, as it could be interpreted to support the corporatist theory of estates. The nobles were meeting spontaneously to defend their corporative rights against those of the clergy. This isolated example is not sufficient, however, to justify wholehearted endorsement of the corporatist theory for the origins of the estates of Poitou.

Alphonse's taxation policy gave rise to a number of assemblies of the nobles of Poitou. He seems to have limited the subsidies he imposed to cases for which it was generally recognized by feudal custom that vassals should make a payment to their lord, such as the knighting of his eldest son, and his own participation in a crusade. In 1241, Alphonse knighted his eldest son and received gifts from various towns, possibly in lieu of a tax. Prior to his participation in the crusade of 1270, he imposed several taxes on different regions of his apanage, including Poitou.[11]

In 1267, he sent commissioners throughout Poitou, Saintonge, and Auvergne seeking voluntary aid for the crusade. They met with very little success.[12] He then imposed a double *cens* on all non-nobles who were directly dependent upon him. He sent commissioners to the towns, however, inviting them to offer a lump sum instead.[13] The towns were reluctant, but finally, under pressure, some of them made offers. Poitiers offered 500 *livres*.[14] Niort refused to bargain and paid the double *cens*.[15]

On September 23, 1268, Alphonse assembled the barons of Poitou in Poitiers to obtain their consent to a tax to be imposed on their sub-

[10] Edgar Boutaric, *Saint Louis et Alphonse de Poitiers* (Paris, 1870), p. 423, hereafter cited as Boutaric.
[11] *Ibid.*, p. 279.
[12] *Correspondance administrative d'Alphonse de Poitiers*, ed. A. Molinier, in *Collection de documents inédits sur l'histoire de France* (Paris, 1894), I, pp. 390-92, nos. 632 and 633, hereafter cited as *Correspondance d'Alphonse de Poitiers*.
[13] Boutaric, p. 285.
[14] *Ibid.*, p. 288.
[15] *Correspondance d'Alphonse de Poitiers*, I, pp. 669-70, no. 1043, Oct. 21, 1269.

jects. They met before three commissioners, Jean de Nanteuil, sire de Tours, Jean de Villette, seneschal of Saintonge, and Eustaches de Beaumarchais, seneschal of Poitou. The nobles only promised at this assembly to come before the count and give him what they saw fit. Alphonse was not satisfied with this reply, but was rather unsure of his rights. The commissioners told him that they knew of no custom requiring the nobles to consent to any tax. Alphonse claimed that other lords in the past had collected *aides* for crusades, and instructed the commissioners to look into the means by which they had done so.[16]

One year later, the barons still had given nothing. Alphonse finally lost patience and ordered the above three commissioners to order the nobles to grant a reasonable sum and to fix a date, after which he would collect it by force.[17] The barons finally voted him 10,000 *livres*.[18]

Before levying the above taxes, Alphonse preferred to consult those concerned, instead of imposing them by force, as he probably had the feudal right to do. He obtained the consent of the towns, not by provincial assemblies, but individually by sending commissioners from town to town. He obtained the consent of the nobles to tax their subjects. This consent was sometimes obtained individually, sometimes in assemblies.[19] Boutaric concludes that Alphonse de Poitiers never summoned the three estates together to vote taxes in any of the lands under his control.[20] It should be noted, however, that he did summon somewhat more restricted assemblies from time to time to advise him on specific matters, as in Agenais in 1252 or 1253 and again in 1263.[21] Also the general court of Agenais, consisting of nobles and townsmen, met frequently during the years when this province formed part of Alphonse's apanage, usually for military or judicial purposes.[22] Also, assemblies of nobles, such as that held in Agenais in 1270, were by no means uncommon in his lands.

One more assembly of the nobles of Poitou, only indirectly connected with taxation, took place under Alphonse de Poitiers. In May 1269,

[16] Boutaric, p. 283. *Correspondance d'Alphonse de Poitiers*, I, pp. 449-50, no. 707.
[17] *Ibid.*, pp. 678-79, nos. 1041 and 1042, letters of Oct. 19, 1269.
[18] *Ibid.*, pp. 698-700, no. 1066.
[19] Boutaric, p. 307.
[20] *Ibid.*, p. 530.
[21] Ferdinand Lot and Robert Fawtier, *Histoire des institutions françaises au moyen âge* (Paris, 1957), I, 95.
[22] For a detailed description of the general court of Agenais during this period see Thomas Bisson, *Assemblies and Representation in Languedoc In The Thirteenth Century* (Princeton, 1964), pp. 73-101.

Alphonse presided over an assembly of the barons of Poitou which settled the *droit de rachat* concerning land inheritance. The barons paid for this settlement.[23] On the death of Alphonse de Poitiers in 1271, Poitou escheated to the crown.

Under Philip III, Philip IV, Louis X, and Philip V, the government generally asked for consent to taxation, but it was not bound to obtain that consent in any specified way. It could negotiate with individuals, towns, *baillages*, or larger regions. Expediency, not constitutional forms, determined the method used.[24]

There seem to be no definite records of assemblies in Poitou to vote taxes during the reign of Philip IV, although it is possible that some took place in 1291. In July of that year Philip the Fair ordered the expulsion of all Jews from the *sénéchaussée* of Poitou on condition that, to compensate him for the taxes paid by them, a tax of six *sous* per hearth (*feu*) be levied annually in the *sénéchaussée*.[25] This tax was definitely imposed. The receipts of the treasurers of the Louvre of November 1296 show that the seneschal of Poitou paid 3300 *livres tournois*, given him by the receiver of a *fouage* for the expulsion of the Jews from Poitou. The document says that the inhabitants of Poitou had consented to this *fouage of* their free will and with the consent of their lords.[26] How this tax was voted is not indicated. It is possible that assemblies of towns and barons took place.

Under Philip V consent to taxation continued to be obtained locally, although in 1318-19 the way was prepared by large assemblies of towns and nobles to agree to the principle of a tax.[27] In 1319, following these large assemblies, the nobles and the towns of Poitou were called upon to furnish money or men for the defense of the Flemish frontier.

The king had convoked three great assemblies of the barons of France in 1318-19.[28] Those from Poitou had been summoned to an assembly in Paris on February 9, 1319. The nobles at this assembly had refused to vote a subsidy, alleging the absence of large numbers of their colleagues whom they wished to consult. The king then summoned seven local assemblies of nobles to obtain the required consent.

---

[23] Boutaric, p. 490.
[24] Strayer and Taylor, pp. 89-90 and 163-67.
[25] *Recueil de documents concernant la commune et la ville de Poitiers*, I, ed. E. Audoin, *A. H. P.*, XLIV, pp. 226-28, no. 147.
[26] *Ibid.*
[27] Strayer and Taylor, pp. 163-67.
[28] Charles M. Taylor, "The Composition of Baronial Assemblies in France, 1315-1320", *Speculum*, XXIX (1954), 441-48.

The time and place of the local assembly of the nobles of Poitou is indicated by a letter from Philip V, dated February 22, 1319, to the viscount of Thouars summoning him and the other nobles of Poitou to assemble at Poitiers on Palm Sunday (March 26) before two royal commissioners, Robert d'Artois and the bishop of Amiens.[29] This letter refers to the earlier assembly at Paris and to the reluctance of the small number of nobles from Poitou who had attended to vote the requested subsidy. The results of this assembly in Poitiers are unknown.

The towns of Poitou were also asked to contribute. On January 5, 1319, the seneschal of Poitou, Regnault Clignet, received an order from the king to assemble the deputies of the towns of the *sénéchaussée*.[30] In order to spare the deputies the expense of travelling, he was instructed to go in person from town to town and assemble the principal inhabitants. According to Berranger, in his extensive study on the administration of Poitou, this is the only case in the period 1271-1361 when the towns of Poitou were summoned to assemble, and even in this case they did not actually meet together.[31] The town of Poitiers granted 500 *livres*, which was to be collected by four delegates of the town council.[32]

For the period 1328-1380, a useful collection of documents has been published concerning the town of Poitiers.[33] This collection includes numerous documents about the levying of taxes, and not one refers to an assembly of the three estates, or even to separate assemblies of the different orders. In each case it was the town of Poitiers that consented to the tax.

In a lengthy introduction to this collection, Boissonnade discusses the methods of levying these taxes.[34] He points out that the town's charter of 1222 stipulated that Poitiers would not be subjected to any taxes to which it had not freely consented. This privilege was not always fully respected, but in general the town council succeeded in maintaining three prerogatives; the right to consent to new taxes, the

[29] *Recueil de documents concernant le Poitou contenus dans les régistres de la Chancellerie de France (1334-1348)*, ed. P. Guérin, *A. H. P.*, XIII (1883), pp. 52-53, hereafter cited as Guérin, *A. H. P.*
[30] *Ibid.*, XI, pp. 190-94.
[31] Henri de Berranger, "La Sénéchaussée de Poitou de la mort d'Alphonse de Poitiers à l'occupation anglaise (1271-1361). Etude sur l'administration royale" (Unpublished Thesis, *Ecole des Chartes*, 1924), p. 68.
[32] A. C. Poitiers, I, 1.
[33] *Recueil de documents concernant la commune et la ville de Poitiers*, II, ed. E. Audouin, *A. H. P.*, XLVI (1928), hereafter cited as Audouin, *Recueil*, II, *A. H. P.*
[34] *Ibid.*, p. XXXIV ff.

right to force all classes to pay, and the right to look after distribution and collection.[35]

The principle of consent to royal taxes was recognized formally in 1329, following a protest by the mayor.[36] Therefore, in 1329, 1337, 1352, 1357, 1373, and 1380, assemblies of bourgeois, clergy, and inhabitants of the town and *châtellenie* of Poitiers met to discuss the voting of taxes.[37]

As a rule during this period, all classes in Poitiers paid taxes. This was the case, for example, in 1329 and 1337.[38] In 1345, when the nobles refused to pay, a royal commissioner authorized the mayor to force them to do so.[39] In 1380, the names of the bishop of Poitiers and other clergymen and nobles appear on the tax roll.[40]

The mayor and bourgeois had the right to apportion taxes in the town, a privilege that was acknowledged in 1329.[41] Royal officials usually apportioned taxes outside the jurisdiction of the commune, as in 1337.[42]

The above evidence for Poitou seems to be in general agreement with the findings of Viard in his study on taxation during the reign of Philip VI.[43] In general, the king announced his intention of imposing a tax for a certain purpose, and then negotiated the amount with the towns, individual nobles, or groups of nobles. Even when the Estates General voted a tax, it was still necessary to negotiate on the local level.[44] Let us examine a few examples of the taxation policy of Philip VI in Poitou.

In 1336 the king was raising money for a projected crusade, and in February of that year he sent commissioners to Niort. The mayor and town of Niort promised to pay eighty *livres* per year for four years if the king went on the crusade in person.[45]

In 1339 the king seems to have held a general assembly of towns to agree to the principle of a tax before turning to local negotiations. On

---

[35] *Ibid.*, pp. LVI-LVII.
[36] *Ibid.*, no. 283.
[37] *Ibid.*, p. LVII.
[38] *Ibid.*, nos. 284, 322.
[39] *Ibid.*, no. 360.
[40] *Ibid.*, no. 479.
[41] *Ibid.*, no. 283.
[42] *Ibid.*, no. 321.
[43] Jules Viard, "Les ressources extraordinaires de la royauté sous Philippe VI de Valois", *Revue des Questions Historiques*, XLIV (1888), 167-218, hereafter cited as Viard, "Les ressources extraordinaires", *R. Q. H.*
[44] *Ibid.*, p. 201.
[45] *Ibid.*, p. 174.

May 8, 1339 a royal order was sent to two royal commissioners instructing them to collect a tax that the towns of Poitou had promised the king to help him sustain his war against the English.[46] The document states that the king had summoned before him delegates from a number of towns, including towns in Poitou, to seek financial aid and that they had agreed. They had apparently not fixed the amount, as the king and council had decided that the same subsidy that had been imposed in the year beginning Ascension 1337 would suffice. The commissioners were instructed to travel around the *sénéchaussée* of Poitou and collect this tax.

In order to obtain the consent of the nobles to a tax being collected in their lands, the king frequently agreed to give them a portion of the tax. For example, in 1342 he shared with Miles de Thouars, sire de Pousauges in Poitou, the receipts from a sales tax of four *deniers* per *livre* imposed in his lands.[47]

A document of September 11, 1349 refers to a tax of twelve *deniers* per *livre* "recently granted to the king our lord in the *sénéchaussée* of Poitou" to pay troops stationed there.[48] How this tax was granted is not indicated.

The departmental archives of Deux-Sèvres contain an order, dated April 18, 1350 by the seneschal of Poitou, the abbot of Saint-Cyprien, and the mayor of Poitiers to the receiver of "a certain *aide*" imposed in Poitou for the expenses of the war to pay to the royal lieutenant in Poitou and Touraine, the sum of four hundred *livres tournois* to pay the soldiers under his command.[49] In spite of an unclear and unsubstantiated statement in the inventory of these archives,[50] there is no reason to believe that this tax was granted by the three estates of Poitou. In view of the complete lack of any reference to the estates of Poitou in other documents of the period, it seems unlikely that they met in 1350, although it is by no means impossible.

During the reign of John the Good there are no indications of as-

---

46   A. C. Poitiers, I, 3.
47   Viard, "Les Ressources extraordinaires", *R. Q. H.*, XLIV, 189.
48   A. N., K K 648, f° 91, no. 83.
49   A. D. Deux-Sèvres, C 17.
50   *Inventaire sommaire des archives départementales des Deux-Sèvres antérieures à 1790*, compiled by Gouget and Dacier, Series C, D, E, F, G, H (Melle, 1896), p. 12, refers to the three men issuing the order as the commission of the Three Estates of Poitiers (not Poitou) of 1350. There is nothing in the document to indicate that this is the case, and the compilers of the inventory cite no other sources to justify their statement.

semblies of the estates of Poitou. Taxes in the area seem to have been imposed on the individual towns. For example, in 1353 Charles d'Espagne, constable of France, ordered a tax of six *deniers* per *livre* to be imposed on the town and *châtellenie* of Poitiers.[51]

The ransom of King John, who was captured by the English at the battle of Poitiers in 1356, gave rise to some assemblies in France. In June 1358, the king appointed commissioners in the various *baillages* and *sénéchaussées* of the kingdom with orders to require the members of all classes to contribute to his ransom.[52] His letter appointing three commissioners for Poitou has survived.[53] They are instructed to force all prelates and clergy, nobles, townsmen and inhabitants of the *sénéchaussée* to pay their share of his ransom. In a few regions of France assemblies of estates met to vote the required sums, but in general the response was apathetic.[54] There is no evidence to indicate that any such assemblies occurred in Poitou. By the treaty of Brétigny in 1360, Poitou was surrendered to the English. It seems to have made no contribution to King John's ransom.

From 1360 to 1372, Poitou was administered by the English as part of the duchy of Aquitaine. During the last ten years of this period, the duchy was governed by the Black Prince. He assembled the three estates of Aquitaine nearly every year, and was granted a *fouage* on almost every occasion. For example, they met in June 1364 at Périgueux, July 1365 at Bordeaux, September 1365 at Périgueux, January 1368 at Angoulême, and June 1368 at Saintes.[55] Very little is known about the composition of these assemblies, but presumably, clergymen, nobles, and townsmen from Poitou and the other provinces in Aquitaine were summoned. There seems to be no record, however, of any taxes voted by the individual provincial estates in this period anywhere in Aquitaine.

It is true that Froissart states that "parlements" were held at Poitiers, Niort, Angoulême, Bordeaux, and Bergerac concerning the *fouage* imposed by the Black Prince in 1368.[56] M. Luce, in editing Froissart's

51   Audouin, *Recueil*, II, *A. H. P.*, XLVI, no. 392.
52   R. Delachenal, *Histoire de Charles V* (Paris, 1909), II, 69, hereafter cited as Delachenal.
53   A. C. Poitiers, I, 6.
54   Delachenal, II, 71.
55   *Ibid.*, IV, 56-61.
56   Jean Froissart, *Chroniques*, pub. Siméon Luce, *Société de l'Histoire de France* (1878), VII, Chapter XCIV, paragraph 601, hereafter cited as Froissart, *Chroniques*.

Chroniques, states his belief that the assemblies at Poitiers, Niort, Bordeaux, and Bergerac were merely preliminary assemblies to elect delegates from these towns to the assemblies of the estates at Angoulême in January 1368 and Saintes in August 1368.[57] Froissart is sometimes vague or inaccurate about such matters, which lacked the colour and pageantry to excite his interest. In any case, there are no other references to any such assemblies, except the meeting at Angoulême where the three estates of Aquitaine voted a *fouage*.

The paucity of documents concerning the administration of the Black Prince in Aquitaine prevents one from expressing absolute certainty, but it is not probable that he summoned assemblies of provincial estates. He modelled his government as closely as possible on that of England, where taxes were voted by Parliament rather than by local assemblies. This may explain in part his preference for the large estates of Aquitaine rather than local provincial estates.

The first assembly for which we have definite proof that representatives of all three estates of Poitou met together was in 1372 in connection with the restoration of the province to French control. On September 18, 1372 various prelates and nobles of Poitou signed an agreement with the duke of Berry at Surgères.[58] A truce was proclaimed to last until November 30. Most of the pro-English nobles of Poitou were in the town of Thouars, which was being besieged by the French. It was agreed that if the town had not been relieved by the English by November 30, it would capitulate. This date passed without the town being relieved. Therefore, on December 1, in accordance with the agreement made at Surgères, various clergy, nobles and others assembled in the church of the *Frères Mineurs* in Loudun and signed a treaty with the duke of Berry, the duke of Burgundy, and the other French commanders, Du Guesclin and de Clisson.[59]

On December 15, 1372, Charles V confirmed this treaty made by these four commanders with "certain prelates, churchmen, barons, lords, ladies, *and others* of Poitou and Saintonge" regarding the return of these provinces to France.[60] A letter of Charles V, dated March 3, 1375 confirming the rights of the duke of Berry in Poitou and other provinces, indicates that the *others* referred to above included representatives of the towns.[61]

---

[57] *Ibid.*, p. XXXV, note 1.
[58] Delachenal, IV, 432-33.
[59] Froissart, *Chroniques*, VIII, pp. CLV-CLIX. Delachenal, IV, 435-36.
[60] B. N. ms. fr. 3910, fol. III. Also Guérin, *A. H. P.*, XIX, 176-90 and 199-205.
[61] *Ibid.*, 367-72. It refers to promises made by the duke of Berry, the duke of

Whether or not this assembly at Loudun should be called a meeting of the estates of Poitou is largely a matter of terminology. Guérin refers to it as such.[62] In any case, it marks an important precedent in the history of the estates of Poitou as, for the first time, so far as we know, all three estates were apparently represented at the same assembly.

When Poitou was recaptured by the French in 1372, it was granted to the duke of Berry as part of his apanage, in which category it remained until his death in 1416. It is during this period that the three estates of Poitou seem to have begun to meet fairly regularly for the first time.

In the years immediately following 1372, the old procedure of taxes being granted by the individual towns rather than by the estates of the province appears to have persisted, however. In 1372, Charles V had declared the town of Poitiers exempt from all taxes for ten years.[63] This exemption was largely adhered to, but a few contributions were demanded. For example, in 1373 the town and *châtellenie* of Poitiers agreed to pay 2000 *livres* for the construction of a fortress at Lusignan, and in 1380 an assembly of the clergy, mayor, and *bourgeois* of Poitiers authorized a *taille* of 1000 *livres* for repairs to the town wall and for the military expenses of the duke of Berry.[64] Although the evidence is not conclusive, it is possible that the three estates of Poitou met in 1375. A letter of Charles V, dated March 26, 1375 granted to the duke of Berry the right to levy a tax of twelve *deniers* per *livre* on all merchandise sold in Poitou for three years "on the condition, however, that the people of the said *pays*, or the largest and wisest portion of them, shall consent to it".[65] M. Teilhard, who published this document, assumed this to mean that the consent of the provincial estates was required.[66] His assumption seems reasonable, and is strengthened by a letter from the duke of Berry, dated June 14, 1375 ordering one of his creditors to be paid from this tax "which had recently been granted to him".[67]

It is likely that a number of assemblies of provincial estates took place in various parts of France towards the close of the year 1380. In November of that year, a large assembly was held at Paris that could

---

Burgundy, and the constable (du Guesclin) to "genz d'église, seigneurs et *communes* du pais de poitou" when they returned to French control.

[62]	*Ibid.*, 176, note 1, and 368, note 2.
[63]	Audouin, *Recueil*, II, *A. H. P.*, XLVI, no. 446.
[64]	*Ibid.*, nos. 445 and 479.
[65]	*Régistre de Barthélemi de Noces, officier du Duc de Berri* (1374-1377), published by E. Teilhard de Chardin, *Bibliothèque de l'Ecole des Chartes*, LII (1891), 517, hereafter cited as *Régistre de Barthélemi de Noces, Bib. Ec. Ch.*
[66]	*Ibid.*, 230.
[67]	*Ibid.*, 554.

perhaps be termed a meeting of the Estates General of Languedoil. The result was the Ordonnance of November 16 abolishing the *aides*. In return for this concession the assembly probably agreed in principle to a tax. M. Mirot believes that the nature and amount of this tax was then decided in assemblies of provincial estates.[68] Very few of the documents have survived, with the exception of the royal letters of November 27 to the *bailli* of Cotentin instructing him to assemble the three estates of Normandy.[69] The letter states that "it has been decided that the clergy, nobles, bourgeois, and other notable persons of each *pays* of our said kingdom shall hold assemblies in their *pays*." The terms of this letter imply that similar assemblies were to be held throughout the kingdom.[70] No documents have survived concerning the estates of Poitou at this time, but it is quite possible that it met.

Very likely numerous assemblies of provincial estates took place in February 1381. Those of Normandy and Chartres definitely met and voted a tax, and there is proof that a similar tax was imposed in other regions. The Ordonnance of March 20, 1381 refers to the tax voted and the means by which it was to be collected.[71] Once again, there is no proof that the estates of Poitou met, but it is quite possible that it did.

In 1381, Poitou and Saintonge were partially in the hands of the English and were being pillaged by armed bands. The duke of Berry passed through the region on his way to put down an insurrection in Languedoc. According to d'Aussy, he paused long enough to assemble the estates of Poitou and Saintonge at Niort to inquire into the situation.[72] The wording of the letter which d'Aussy cites as proof does not make clear the nature of the assembly, but it was very probably, as he believes, a meeting of the three estates of these two provinces.[73]

An interesting document proves almost conclusively that the estates of Poitou met in about 1382.[74] It is dated May 22, 1383, and describes

---

[68] Léon Mirot, "Les Etats généraux et provinciaux et l'abolition des aides au début du règne de Charles VI", *Revue des Questions Historiques, LXXIV* (1903), 398 ff., hereafter cited as Mirot, "Les Etats généraux et provinciaux", *R. Q. H.*, LXXIV.

[69] B. N., ms. fr. 20,584, no. 41.

[70] Mirot, "Les Etats généraux et provinciaux", *R. Q. H.*, LXXIV, 433.

[71] *Ibid.*, 438-44.

[72] Denys d'Aussy, "La Saintonge pendant la Guerre de Cent Ans", *Bulletin de la Société des A. H. S. A.*, XIV (1894), 221.

[73] Letter of April 27, 1381, from the Constable Olivier de Clisson to the mayor of Saint-Jean d'Angély summoning him to attend this meeting. *Régistres de l'Echevinage de Saint-Jean d'Angély (1332-1496)*, pub. D. d'Aussy, *A. H. S. A.*, XXIV (1895), 258-59.

[74] A. N., X 1C 46B, no. 207.

a case before the Parlement of Paris between Louis, viscount of Rochechouart and his wife on the one hand, and the duke of Berry on the
other. The complaint of the former was against Etienne Daniel, receiver
for the duke of Berry, and against two men commissioned by Daniel.
The plaintiffs claimed that they held the viscounty of Rochechouart from
the duke of Berry, as well as other lands in Poitou, and that in these
lands they had all powers of justice, high, middle and low. Nevertheless,
Daniel had sent two commissioners to force the subjects of Rochechouart
and his wife to pay a *fouage* of fifteen *francs* per parish to the duke of
Berry. These commissioners had attempted to do so without consulting
either Rochechouart and his wife or their officials, although the plaintiffs had not consented to this tax. They acknowledged that a certain
grant had been made to the duke of Berry by "aucuns des nobles du
clergie et des bourgs du pays de poitou". However, they declared that it
had been expressly stipulated that this tax would be collected by the
seigneurs of the province, each in his own lands, or by their officials,
and that each *seigneur* would retain one third of the amount collected
in his lands. Rochechouart and his wife had duly presented their case
before the *Parlement*. The court's decision cannot be determined.

In addition to describing the first definite case of the three estates of
Poitou voting a tax, the document throws valuable light on the methods
by which such taxes were collected at this period. In this case, it was to
be collected by the *seigneurs* in their own lands, and they were to retain
a share of it in return for their consent to its being imposed upon their
subjects.

Another interesting point may possibly be deduced from this case.
The viscount of Rochechouart and his wife complained that the tax
was being collected in their lands although they had not consented to it.
Perhaps they were not only complaining about the means of collection
but also because they did not feel themselves bound by the vote of an
assembly that they had not attended. If this is the case, then it would
indicate that the institution of provincial estates had not yet evolved to
the point where its vote clearly obligated all members of each estate,
whether they attended or not. This would suggest that the element of
personal consent was still predominant and that obtaining consent to a
tax in an assembly of the three estates was still nothing more than a
convenient way of obtaining the individual consent of those concerned.

Documents concerning Poitou during the 1380's are extremely scarce,
and it is not possible to indicate any further assemblies of the estates of
the province during this period. After 1390, as will be seen, we have

proof that they met fairly regularly. It may well be that they were also meeting regularly during the 1380's but, if so, the documents concerning them have not survived.

To sum up, the separate assemblies of the nobles and of the towns of Poitou in the thirteenth and early fourteenth centuries, as well as the synods of the clergy of the dioceses of the region, seem to have been preliminary steps in the development of the estates of Poitou. This development did not reach its completion as early in Poitou as in some other areas. In fact, from 1319 to 1372, there are no records of any such assemblies at all. Throughout most of this fifty-three year period, the situation in Poitou was very unstable, as much of the fighting between the English and the French took place in this region and the province was constantly being pillaged by soldiers of both sides. This may in part explain the slow development of the estates. Another possibility is that some separate assemblies of the nobles or towns did take place but that the documents concerning them were destroyed in the constant lootings and burnings. During the brief period of the English control from 1360 to 1372, no assemblies of clergy or nobles or towns, separately or together, seem to have taken place, although once again the scarcity of documents prevents one from expressing absolute certainty on this point.

Finally, in the 1370's and the 1380's, when Poitou had returned to French control, the duke of Berry began to summon the three estates of Poitou. Thus he brought to sudden completion the gradual process of development of this institution whose early stages can be seen in the thirteenth and early fourteenth centuries, but whose development seems to have lapsed for fifty or sixty years. In so doing, he may have been influenced by existing institutions in Auvergne and Berry, the other parts of his apanage.

Having traced the development of the estates of Poitou through its preliminary stages down to the period when the three orders began to meet together frequently, let us now see which, if either, of the two theories of origins described at the beginning of this chapter is applicable. In general, the evidence for Poitou seems to support the theory that provincial estates developed from the feudal council and from the duty of a vassal to provide his lord with aid and advice (*auxilium et consilium*).

With two exceptions, every known assembly of one or more of the three orders that took place in Poitou during the thirteenth and fourteenth centuries was summoned by the feudal lord of Poitou. When the province was part of the royal domain, they were summoned by the king. When it formed part of the apanage of a great lord, they were summoned by the lord. The two exceptions are the assembly of the nobles of Poitou in November 1246, and the assembly of clergy, nobles, and towns of Poitou on December 1, 1372. In the first case, the nobles assembled spontaneously to defend their rights against the clergy. This assembly, as indicated above,[75] could be interpreted to support the corporatist theory for the origins of estates. Although this is an isolated case, the corporatist theory cannot be entirely rejected. Much more evidence, however, seems to support the feudal council theory. The assembly of December 1, 1372 was summoned by the French commanders who had reconquered the area to arrange for the return of Poitou and Saintonge to the allegiance of the king of France. This is an exceptional case. As the purpose of the assembly was precisely to settle the matter of the feudal overlordship of Poitou, which was temporarily in doubt, it is obvious that it could not possibly have been summoned by the feudal lord. Every other assembly in Poitou in the thirteenth and fourteenth centuries was summoned by the feudal lord; the king when it was part of the royal domain, as in 1319; Alphonse de Poitiers and John, duke of Berry, when Poitou formed part of their apanage.[76]

Again excluding the two assemblies of November 1246 and December 1, 1372, every assembly during this period was either an example of a meeting of the feudal council in its plenary sense or of the feudal obligation to render aid and advice to one's lord. The assembly of nobles of May 1269, to settle the matter of the *droit de rachat*, was clearly an example of the lord and his council acting in a judicial capacity. Alphonse de Poitiers was settling in his court a legal point concerning his vassals about which they were in doubt. When John, duke of Berry, assembled the estates of Poitou in 1381 to give him information on the troubled situation in the area, he was acting as a lord seeking counsel (*consilium*). Every other assembly during the period was for the purpose of voting a tax. This might be interpreted as an aspect of the obligation to provide one's lord with aid (*auxilium*).

It does not seem necessary to adopt the explanation of the corporatists to explain why, as these assemblies developed from the feudal council,

---

[75] Above, p. 21.
[76] Actually, the assemblies of the estates of Poitou in November 1390 and November 1391, were summoned by the count of Montpensier, son of the duke of Berry, presumably with his father's authorization.

they were subdivided into three separate orders or estates. It was merely a case of following the customary divisions of medieval society. Ever since the development of feudalism, society had been divided into three fairly distinct groups with, according to medieval thinking, three distinct functions in life. These groups were the clergy, the nobles, and the non-nobles; those who prayed, those who fought, and those who worked. The latter group remained voiceless for some time but, with the rise of the towns in the eleventh and twelfth centuries, and of a wealthy middle class within them, this one part of the non-noble group reached a point where its aid and counsel were of value, and it appeared as the third estate. As privileged towns appeared in his territory, the lord invited them to attend the deliberations of his vassals. The towns were thus introduced into a previously existing assembly.[77] The peasants remained voiceless unless they were, as some historians believe, represented in theory by their lords. Hence, as the assemblies developed from the feudal council, they were subdivided into these three social groups which, at first, usually met separately. It was only gradually that the practice of assembling them all together at the same time and in the same place was adopted.

While the feudal council theory seems the most suitable to explain the origins of the estates of Poitou, it is necessary to make three qualifying remarks. In the first place, the assembly of nobles of November 1246 makes possible a corporatist theory of origins. In the second place, the paucity of documents concerning assemblies in Poitou during the thirteenth and fourteenth centuries means that the conclusions are based on somewhat limited evidence. In the third place, the light thrown by the estates of Poitou on the problem of the origins of provincial estates is limited to some extent by its relatively late development and by the fact that, in the final stages of this development, it may have been influenced by the previously existing estates of Berry and Auvergne.

As Dupont-Ferrier has pointed out,[78] it is probably a mistake to look for identical origins for all of the provincial estates of France. Nevertheless, the theory that they developed from the feudal council and from the obligation of the vassal to provide his lord with *auxilium* and *consilium* explains the origins of quite a number of them including, in spite of the above qualifications, the estates of Poitou.

---

[77] This is shown by the corporatist Emile Lousse, "Assemblées d'Etats", *Etudes*, VII, 242. It is perfectly compatible with the feudal council theory as well.

[78] Dupont-Ferrier, "De quelques problèmes", *Journal des Savants* (Aug.-Oct. 1928), pp. 318-19.

II

FUNCTIONS AND ACTIVITIES

A. FINANCIAL[1]

During the years of their most frequent meetings, the chief functions of
the three estates of Poitou were financial in nature. This financial activity
was confined almost entirely to the period c. 1390 to c. 1470, and was
most important during the years prior to 1435.[2]

The principal function of the estates of Poitou from the time of its
origins until about 1435 was to vote taxes to its feudal lord. As Poitou
reverted to the royal domain in 1422, all taxes after that date were voted
to the king. Every meeting of the three estates of the province between
1382 and 1412 was for the purpose of granting a tax.[3] At twelve of
the twenty-three definite meetings between November 1412 and 1435 a
tax was voted. The purpose of four other assemblies cannot be ascertained and at some of them taxes may also have been granted.

The amount voted varied from 10,000 *livres tournois* granted to the
count of Montpensier in 1390, and again in 1391, to 60,000 *livres
tournois* to the king on the occasion of his coronation in the latter half
of 1429. In 1435 the three estates of Poitou assembled and voted a direct
tax in lieu of the indirect *aide* that had been granted by the Estates
General of Languedoil in January of that year. This is the last time for
many years that we have definite evidence of the estates of Poitou meet-

[1] This section, in its essentials, has already appeared in *Mediaeval Studies*, XXVI
(1964), 186 ff. It is here somewhat revised, particularly the parts dealing with the
activity of the *élus*.
[2] The only activity of the estates of Poitou after 1470 which might be considered
financial in nature occurred between the years 1549 and 1553 when it met several
times with the estates of neighbouring provinces to protest to the king about the
gabelle and other salt taxes. These meetings will be discussed in section C. of this
chapter.
[3] For the sources for any references in this chapter to specific assemblies of the
estates of Poitou, see Appendix A, Catalogue of Assemblies, under the appropriate
date.

ing to consent to royal taxes.[4] Henceforth it appears that the king imposed taxes directly in Poitou through the royal *élus* without consulting the three estates.[5] Thomas' contention that never, from 1418 to 1451, did Charles VII levy a direct tax without the participation of the provincial estates [6] cannot be substantiated in the case of Poitou.

A subject that merits a special study is the relationship between the voting of taxes by the Estates General and the voting of taxes by provincial estates during the early part of the reign of Charles VII. The principal question is, did the provincial estates normally meet after the Estates General had granted a royal tax to agree to their provinces' share of this tax? Some historians, much as Laferrière,[7] believe that this was the usual procedure. The evidence in the case of Poitou is inconclusive however.

On November 1, 1424, the three estates of Poitou voted 50,000 *livres tournois* as that province's share of one million *livres* granted to the king by the Estates General at Poitiers in the previous month. This is the only occasion where it can be definitely established that this procedure was followed. Late in 1425, the three estates of Poitou met immediately following the assembly of the Estates General held in Poitiers in October and voted a small additional sum over and above the province's share of the royal tax. The document describing this meeting states that the king had ordered the main sum to be imposed as Poitou's share of the general tax. There is nothing to show whether or not the estates of Poitou was called upon to consent to this share. Royal letters of May 2, 1433 instructed the *élus des aides* in Poitou to impose a sum of 68,000 *livres tournois* as the provinces' share of a tax granted the king by the Estates General.[8] There is no information available on this supposed meeting of the Estates General, and nothing to show that the three estates of Poitou voted their share. In September or October 1433 the Estates General of Languedoil met at Tours. Hugh, bishop of Poitiers, later acknowledged that he had received 400 *livres tournois* granted him

---

[4] Only twice again, as far as can be determined, did the estates of Poitou have anything to do with voting a royal tax. In 1454 they once again voted a direct tax in lieu of *aides*, and in January 1464 the province was represented at a large regional assembly called to grant a tax to Louis XI.

[5] For the relationship between the *élus* and the estates of Poitou, see below, pp. 46-50.

[6] Thomas, *Les Etats provinciaux*, 69-70.

[7] F. Laferrière, "Etude sur l'histoire et l'organisation comparée des états provinciaux aux diverses époques de la monarchie jusqu'en 1789", *Séances et Travaux de l'Académie des Sciences Morales et Politiques* (Paris, 1860-62), LIII, 115-16.

[8] A. N., K63, no. 25.

by "those of the said *pays* (Poitou) who were at the said assembly." [9]
This sum was to be paid from Poitou's portion of the tax granted at this
meeting. There is nothing to indicate whether or not the estates of Poitou
had anything to say about the size of their portion of the tax. The
wording of the document even seems to imply that the money voted to
the bishop was granted by the delegates from Poitou at the assembly of
the Estates General, rather than by the estates of Poitou. If so, this
was an unusual procedure.

It is apparent then that the evidence as to whether or not the three
estates of Poitou customarily voted that province's share of the taxes
granted by the Estates General is inconclusive. On at least one occasion they did, but it seems probable that this procedure was not always
followed.

The next question to be examined is whether or not the estates of
Poitou had anything to say about the province's share of royal taxes
after the Estates General and the Estates of Languedoil lost the privilege
of voting them. In March 1438, the king imposed a *taille* of 200,000
livres tournois on Languedoil without the consent of the Estates
General or the Estates of Languedoil. Poitou's share was 52,000 *livres*.[10]
In January 1446, a *taille* of 226,000 *livres* was imposed on Languedoil.
Royal letters of April 8, 1446 refer to Poitou's portion of this tax, without specifying its amount.[11] In January 1447, a *taille* of 200,000 *livres
tournois* was imposed on Languedoil. Poitou's share is referred to in a
number of documents, without its amount being stated.[12] There is
nothing to indicate that the estates of the province was consulted on any
of these occasions. It seems then that when the king imposed taxes on
Languedoil without the consent of the Estates General or the Estates
of Languedoil, as he did regularly after 1436 (except in 1439), he and
his officials arbitrarily fixed Poitou's share without consulting the three
estates of the province.

One financial activity in which the estates of Poitou did participate
during the reign of Charles VII was the voting of a direct tax on several
occasions to replace indirect *aides*. Indirect taxes seem to have been
unpopular in fifteenth century France, and direct taxes preferred. This
was partly because indirect taxes were "farmed out" and then rather
dishonestly collected. Also, the people preferred to know in advance

9   B. N., ms. fr. 20,886, fol. 113.
10   *Ibid.*, 21,428, fol. 12, and 23,909, fol. 1.
11   *Ibid.*, p.o. vol. 2374, Précigny, doss. 53,271, no. 12.
12   *Ibid.*, vol. 3041, Vousy, doss. 67,419, no. 6; *Ibid.*, ms. fr. 32,511, fol. 133r°;

precisely what they had to pay. With a direct tax which had been voted by the estates, they knew where they stood. On a number of occasions, the king yielded to popular demand and replaced indirect taxes with a direct tax in various provinces, or even in the whole of Languedoil, as in April 1426.[13] The estates of Poitou at least three times persuaded the king to make this change. Late in 1423, it voted a direct tax of 30,000 *livres tournois* in lieu of the indirect *aide* which had been granted to the king by the Estates General at Selles in August of that year. In 1435 it voted an annual sum of 61,500 *livres* for four years in lieu of the *aides* that had been reestablished for a four year period by the Estates General of Languedoil in January of that year. In April or May 1454, the three estates of Poitou met and decided to request the king to replace the *aides* that had been imposed annually since 1451 by an equivalent direct tax, or *taille*. They decided to send a delegation to the king but delayed doing so because of a rumor that he was coming soon to Poitiers. When the rumor proved to be false they met again on July 18. On September 11, their delegation set out for Bridoré in Touraine where they presented their request to the king.[14] His reply is not known.

So far we have been concerned specifically with the granting of taxes by the three estates of Poitou to their feudal lord. After the province became part of the royal domain, they also frequently voted an additional amount, over and above the royal tax, to be used for local expenses and to cover payments to royal commissioners, royal officials, and various other dignitaries. This sum was usually referred to in the documents as "frais outre le principal", or simply "frais".

From the beginning of the reign of Charles VII until the year 1435 the three estates of Poitou normally voted this additional sum at the same meeting at which they granted the main tax. For example, at an assembly late in 1423 at which they voted 30,000 *livres tournois* to the king in lieu of indirect *aides* they also voted an additional sum of 3700 *livres tournois* "oultre le principal". From this sum the estates stipulated that the two royal commissioners would receive specified amounts. They also decreed that a number of other dignitaries would receive amounts ranging from 100 to 500 *livres* to reimburse them in part for their expenses at the assembly. On November 1, 1424, the three estates of

---

Ibid., ms. fr., n.a. 3624, no. 369; *Ibid.*, ms. fr. 6200, p. 229; A. N., KK 648, fol. 91, no. 84.
[13] A. Thomas, "Les Etats Généraux Sous Charles VII", *Revue Historique*, XL (1889), 62-63.
[14] A. C. Poitiers, J 1206-1207.

Poitou voted the substantial additional sum of 16,000 *livres tournois* over and above the 50,000 *livres* that they had granted as the provinces share of a tax recently granted the king by the Estates General. Out of this additional sum various amounts were to be paid to a number of dignitaries. In October or November 1425, and again in September 1430, when voting a royal tax, the estates of Poitou also voted additional *frais*. From these sums grants were made to a number of persons, most of them royal officials.

Several of these grants are of interest! In September 1430, Geoffrey, lord of Mareuil, counsellor and royal Chamberlain, seneschal of Saintonge, was to receive 800 *livres* to compensate him in part for his expenses in maintaining a *bastide* before his castle of Mareuil, which was occupied at the time by the English. This shows that these grants were not necessarily limited to covering the expenses of royal officials and notables incurred in attending the meetings of the estates. In August or September 1434, the three estates of Poitou granted the seneschal of the province, Jean de la Roche, 4000 *livres tournois* to beseige a certain fortress and to stop pillaging. Of this sum, 2000 *livres* was to be imposed over and above the principal of a tax granted at a joint assembly in August of the provincial estates of Poitou, Saintonge, Anjou, and Touraine. The remaining 2000 *livres* was to be paid from the next tax to be levied by the king in Poitou. De la Roche and his men were to cease imposing various charges on the province and return everything that they had seized. They were also to drive out various Scottish bands, as well as the men of a certain local noble, Symmonet de la Touche. The king gave his approval to this arrangement. On November 4, 1434, de la Roche acknowledged receipt of the first 2000 *livres* of this sum. During the first half of 1435, when voting a direct tax of 61,500 *livres tournois* per year in lieu of *aides*, the estates of Poitou also voted an extra sum of 1125 *livres*. Part of this amount was to be used for the usual grants to the royal commissioners and other notables. The other part was to cover payments to the bishop of Poitiers, the lord of Gaucourt, Le Galoys du Puy du Fou, and Jean Chastenier for their expenses incurred in a trip to impose a tax and borrow money to be used to clear various armed bands out of Poitou.

Between the spring of 1436 and the spring of 1445, only one assembly of the three estates of Poitou can be discovered. They were no longer asked to consent to the royal tax, and they seem temporarily to have ceased voting the *frais* as well. In March 1438, for example, the king imposed a tax of 52,000 *livres* on Poitou as their share of a general *taille* to be levied in Languedoil.[15] He also stipulated that various additional sums were to be paid, including 2875 *livres* for the queen's expenses and for payments to royal councillors, and 2915 *livres* for *"frais"*. There is nothing to indicate that the consent of the estates of Poitou was sought. A letter from Charles VII, dated March 2, 1442, to the *élus* in Poitou instructed them to impose the sum of 1650 *livres tournois* "over and above the principal of the next *aide* which is levied in our said *pays* of Poitou".[16] This sum was to be paid to Charles of Anjou to help him meet his expenses in the royal service. As the king specified the amount of the *frais* even before the amount of the tax itself had been decided upon, it seems unlikely that the consent of the three estates of the province was sought. Thomas found that, in the provinces he studied, the king restricted the right of the provincial estates to vote *frais* after about 1440, and that henceforth royal letters patent were required.[17] In Poitou the royal policy seems to have been similar.

In March 1445, the three estates of Poitou entered upon a nine year period of renewed activity. They do not seem to have consented to royal taxes during this period,[18] but they did once again vote *frais*. The account of Jean de Xaincoins, receiver general of all finances for Languedoil and Languedoc, for the year ending September 1446 contains a number of references to specific sums voted by the three estates of Poitou to various dignitaries, including the dauphin and Pierre de Brézé, a well-known royal advisor who was seneschal of Poitou at the time. In January 1447 the king imposed a *taille* of 200,000 *livres* on Languedoil. Although Poitou's share of this tax was fixed arbitrarily by royal officials, the three estates of the province did vote an additional sum for grants to various notables, including the bishop of Poitiers and Pierre de Brézé.

In late 1446, or early 1447, the king agreed to free the province from a royal investigation of crimes and abuses committed by local officials. He issued letters of pardon in which he mentioned some of the crimes which were to have been investigated. One of them is of special interest. He said that sometimes certain officials had collected sums of money

---

[15] B. N., ms. fr. 21,428, fol. 12, and 23,909, fol. 1.
[16] A. N., K67, no. 10.
[17] Thomas, *Les Etats provinciaux*, p. 106.
[18] In 1445 the king imposed a new tax known as the *taille des gens de guerre* in addition to the regular *taille*. Both taxes were then levied annually until 1451, when the regular *taille* was dropped. In some provinces the three estates voted the *taille des gens de guerre*. This leads one to wonder if the renewed activity of the estates of Poitou in 1445 was due to their being summoned to consent to this tax. While the possibility cannot be ruled out entirely, it must be considered im-

along with the *tailles*, without having express authorization to do so, and without notifying the king. They had thus raised large sums, "calling them *frais* or otherwise". That the king considered this an offense showed that he was indeed attempting to clamp down upon the practice of the voting of *frais* by provincial estates. The three estates of Poitou continued to vote small special sums to pay royal officals, but it is likely that, henceforth, specific royal authorization was required. The account of the receiver general of Languedoil and Languedoc for the year ending September 1448 shows two grants by the estates of Poitou to royal officials, one of them to Pierre de Brézé. Probably special royal consent was necessary for these grants, although the document makes no mention of it.

From July 1454 to the death of Charles VII in 1461 there is nothing to indicate that the estates of Poitou met at all. Royal taxes were imposed arbitrarily, and the estates of the province does not seem even to have voted the *frais*. Whether or not it voted *frais* at any of the five assemblies held between August 1461 and August 1466 cannot be ascertained. Three brief references in the annual accounts of the receiver general for Languedoil show, however, that it did so between 1466 and 1470. In fact these three references are all that indicate the continued existence of the estates of Poitou during the four year period. The receiver general's accounts for the years ending September 30, 1467 and September 30, 1468 show 600 *livres tournois* granted in each of these years to Louis de Crussol seneschal of Poitou, by the "inhabitants" of that province. In both cases it is stated that this was with the consent of the king. The receiver general's account for the year ending September 30, 1470 shows a further 600 *livres* granted to Louis de Crussol by the "Estats de Poitou".

Apparently in the late 1460's the three estates of Poitou still retained the right to vote these small additional sums over and above the royal taxes, even though long ago they had lost the privilege of voting the taxes themselves.[19] Also, instead of voting these *frais* freely, as they had in the 1420's and 1430's, they now required special royal permission. After 1470 the royal accounts make no further mention of any grants

---

probable in view of the complete absence of references to such activity on the part of the estates of Poitou in any documents royal or local, including the detailed and valuable Régistres de Poitiers.

[19] Thomas found that, in Auvergne, even after the provincial estates had lost the right to vote royal taxes, they did sometimes, with special royal consent, vote small additional sums for local use. Thomas, *Les Etats provinciaux*, pp. 170-71.

to royal officials by the estates of Poitou, leading one to believe that Louis XI finally deprived it of even this minor privilege.

Closely related to the *frais* were a number of special taxes voted from time to time by the estates of Poitou for specific purposes. In fact the only real difference between these grants and *frais* is the procedural technicality that the latter were always granted at the same time as a direct royal tax, while these special taxes were voted separately at a meeting summoned for that purpose alone.

For example, during the first half of the fifteenth century the estates of Poitou several times granted sums to military commanders for specific campaigns. In August 1404, it probably voted a *fouage* to constable Albret for the seige of Courbefy. In March 1406, it granted a *fouage* to de Torsay, de Harpedenne, and other French commanders to retake Brantôme, Carlux, and Limeuil. In 1409, according to one historian, it voted a *fouage* to constable Albret for a campaign in Périgord. In 1433, the estates of Poitou and Saintonge, meeting jointly, voted Jean de la Roche, seneschal of Poitou, 4000 *livres* to besiege Aubeterre, which was held by the English. By August 1434, however, de la Roche had not received the amount promised. Hence the estates of Poitou agreed that he should receive 1000 *livres tournois* from the principal of a tax just voted at a joint assembly of the estates of several provinces in Tours, plus another 2000 *livres* to be imposed over and above this principal. Presumably the other 1000 *livres* would come from Saintonge. De la Roche acknowledged receipt of 2000 *livres* of this sum on November 4, 1434.[20]

In the spring of 1436 the three estates of Poitou met and voted a tax to raise money for a special gift. Royal letters of April 27, 1436, state that the king had heard that "certain prelates, clergymen, nobles, bourgeois, and inhabitants of certain of the good towns of Poitou" had decided to present the dauphin with various silver dishes on the day of his marriage to Margaret of Scotland. To pay for this, they had voted a tax of 2300 *livres* to be imposed in Poitou over and above their portion of the *taille* granted by the Estates of Languedoil in February. In order to be sure to have the money quickly enough, they wanted to borrow it from certain wealthy citizens, who would be repaid when the tax had been collected. The king agreed, and instructed the *élus* to collect the money in the manner requested. The receiver, Jean Gilier, acknowledged receipt of this 2300 *livres* on June 20, 1436.[21]

20 B. N., Collection Clairambault, 194, fol. 7691.
21 B. N., p.o. vol. 1324, Gilier, doss. 29,964, no. 22.

Another special grant of considerable interest was made by the estates of Poitou in late 1446 or early 1447. In 1446, Charles VII sent the treasurer of France, Jean Bureau, as a commissioner to Poitou to investigate "crimes and excesses" committed by various inhabitants of the province in such matters as the administration of justice and the control of finance.[22] The three estates of Poitou offered the king 18,000 *livres tournois* to be freed from this investigation. The king agreed, and by letters patent of May 24, 1447, named three royal commissioners to raise this tax.[23] They named a receiver, and his accounts show that he collected 21,649 *livres*.[24] The king then granted general letters of pardon, dated March 1447, to any inhabitants of Poitou for any of the carefully enumerated crimes or offenses, in return for this grant.[25]

It is perhaps of interest to examine now briefly several procedural questions in connection with the financial activities of the estates of Poitou. First there is the matter of the apportionment and collection of the taxes it had voted. There the estates seems to have played no part whatsoever. These matters were entirely in the hands of ducal or royal officials. The procedure by which a tax of 10,000 *écus* (about 12,500 *livres tournois*) was apportioned in September and October 1412 is interesting as information of this type is rare for Poitou in the fifteenth century.[26] The tax had been granted to John, duke of Berry, by the three estates of the province on September 29 to meet a threatened English invasion. The duke named a receiver, Maurice Claveurier, and four commissioners. The commissioners divided the sum to be collected among four financial districts, Poitiers, Niort, Thouars, and Fontenay-le-Comte.[27] Then in each of these districts local commissioners, under the supervision of the four general commissioners, apportioned the districts' share amongst the towns, *châtellenies*, and finally the parishes. Each parish was assessed according to a previously fixed number of

---

[22] L. de la Boutetière, "Rôle des tailles en Poitou au XVe siècle", *M. S. A. O.*, Ser. 2, II (1878-79), 502, hereafter cited as La Boutetière, "Rôle des tailles", *M. S. A. O.*, II.

[23] *Ibid.*

[24] B. N., ms. fr. 20,887, fol. 1; *A. H. P.*, XXXI, 117-81.

[25] *Ibid.*, XIX, 413-18.

[26] R. Lacour, "Une Incursion anglaise en Poitou en novembre 1412. Compte d'une aide de 10,000 écus accordée au Duc de Berry pour résister à cette incursion", *A. H. P.*, XLVIII, 1-87, hereafter cited as Lacour, "Une Incursion anglaise", *A. H. P.*, XLVIII. The historian of the field, constantly frustrated by the fragmentary nature of the documents available, cannot help but envy Lacour his good fortune in discovering this detailed description in B. N., ms. fr. 6747, fol. 2 r°.

[27] It was apportioned as follows: Poitiers, 2384 *écus*; Niort, 2996 *écus*, Thouars, 1789 *écus*, Fontenay-le-Comte, 3268 *écus*.

hearths (*feux*). The tax was to be paid by all inhabitants of Poitou except nobles, clergy, and beggars. The money was collected in each of the four main towns by a lieutenant of the receiver closely supervised by the local commissioners and by the four general commissioners. In Poitiers, Claveurier collected personally. The other lieutenants then went to Poitiers and rendered their accounts to Claveurier, who in turn rendered a general account for the entire tax to the ducal *Chambre des Comptes*. Several nobles resisted the collection of the tax in their lands from their peasants as this would obviously reduce their own potential revenues. Only one, the lord of Montaigne, had any success, managing to keep 130 *écus* of the 175 *écus* for which his lands had been assessed. He still had not given it up when Claveurier submitted his accounts. All told, 10,272 *écus* was collected. From this amount, Claveurier deducted 200 *écus* to pay the commissioners and himself. The duke of Berry used most of the remainder to raise troops and to negotiate with the English. The estates of Poitou had nothing to do with any of this process of apportionment and collection.

In November 1424, the procedure for the collection of a tax of 50,000 *livres tournois* in Poitou was similar to that described above. This tax had been voted on November 1, by the three estates of Poitou as the province's share of one million *livres* granted to the king by the Estates General of Languedoil. Once again, four royal commissioners were appointed.[28] The tax was apportioned between the same four financial districts as in 1412, and in general the entire procedure was the same. Once again the estates of Poitou played no part in the apportionment or collection.

On one or two occasions, however, the three estates of Poitou seem to have requested a special procedure for the collection of a tax. This was the limit of their participation, and, even if the king agreed to their request, royal officials handled the entire process. For example, as mentioned already, in the spring of 1436, when they voted 2300 *livres* to buy a wedding gift for the dauphin, the three estates of Poitou proposed that the money be borrowed from various wealthy citizens who were to be paid when the tax was collected. The purpose was to make sure that they had the money in time. The king agreed, but royal officials handled the entire collection of this sum without any participation by the estates. It is possible that the estates of Poitou also recommended a special

---

[28] R. Lacour, "Documents sur les Etats Généraux de Poitiers de 1424 et 1425", *A. H. P.*, XLVIII, 91-117, hereafter cited as Lacour, "Documents sur les Etats Généraux", *A. H. P.*, XLVIII.

method of collection at one of their earliest meetings in 1383. Some years later, in a legal case before the Parlement of Paris, the viscount of Rochechouart claimed that the estates of Poitou, when voting a *fouage* at this assembly, had declared that each *seigneur* should keep one third of the amount collected in his lands.[29]

When voting regular taxes to its feudal lord, king or otherwise, the estates of Poitou seems to have had nothing to say about the use to which the money was put. This, of course, did not apply to special grants, such as the money for the wedding gift to the dauphin in 1436, or the money voted to the king in late 1446 or early 1447 to free the province from a royal investigation of various crimes and misdoings.

The estates of Poitou does not appear to have played any part in the choosing of a receiver or commissioners charged with raising a tax. In September and October 1412, the duke of Berry appointed the receiver and four commissioners, and all of them were ducal officials.[30] The receiver, Maurice Claveurier, was the duke's secretary. The commissioners, Guillaume Taveau, Anceaume le Corgne, Guillaume de Lerberie, and Jean Macé, were all ducal councillors. Taveau was at the same time his Chamberlain and Macé was his receiver of ordinary revenues (such as regular feudal dues) in Poitou.

The payment of the receiver and commissioners who collected taxes does not appear to have been a function of the estates of Poitou while the province was part of the apanage of John, duke of Berry. In November 1390, the commissioners were paid by the receiver out of the main sum voted the count of Montpensier (son of the duke of Berry) by the estates of Poitou.[31] Following the grant of 10,000 *écus* to the duke of Berry on September 29, 1412, the receiver and four commissioners were paid from the main sum of the tax, without any extra money being voted for this purpose by the estates.[32] The receiver, Maurice Claveurier, paid himself 100 *écus*, and paid the four commissioners 25 *écus* each.

During the reign of Charles VII, however, the voting of money for payments to the royal commissioners and other dignitaries seems to have become a frequent function of the three estates of Poitou. It is possible that such payments were in addition to salaries granted them by the king. As seen already, the estates developed the practice of voting additional sums over and above the principal of the royal tax for just such

[29] A. N., X1c 46 B., no. 207.
[30] Lacour, "Une Incursion anglaise", *A. H. P.*, XLVIII, 1-87.
[31] Benjamin Fillon, ed., *Documents pour servir à l'histoire du Bas Poitou*, I (Fontenay-le-Comte, 1847).
[32] Lacour, "Une Incursion anglaise", *A. H. P.*, XLVIII, 1-87.

purposes as this. For example, in December 1423, in addition to a *taille* granted in lieu of indirect taxes, it voted a sum of 3700 *livres* for "frais". From this additional sum, it specified that two of the commissioners, Jean de Torsay, grand master of crossbowmen, and Nicolas de la Barre, royal councillor and *maître des requêtes* of the king's household, would receive 500 *livres* and 100 *livres* respectively.[33]

How long the estates of Poitou continued to vote money to pay the royal commissioners cannot be established precisely. In all probability, it continued to do so until about 1435, when it ceased to vote royal taxes. After this the commissioners seem to have been entirely replaced by the *élus* in the collection of taxes in Poitou.

The role of the *élus* and the relationship between their appearance in a province and the activity of the local estates are matters that merit special examination. As already explained, the arbitrary division of France into *pays d'états* and *pays d'élection* is not valid until at least the late fifteenth century. In the fourteenth and fifteenth centuries nearly every province in France had active estates. This did not necessarily mean that they were free from the activity of the royal *élus*. Many provinces were what Dupont-Ferrier calls "pays d'états à élections",[34] and the appearance of royal *élus* in a province did not necessarily bring about the immediate disappearance of the estates. It is only in the latter part of the reign of Charles VII, when the estates of many provinces lost the right to vote taxes, that the *élus* in these areas took over completely the functions with regard to taxation previously exercised chiefly by the estates and temporarily appointed commissioners.

The earliest mention of *élus* in Poitou that Dupont-Ferrier could find was on November 20, 1403.[35] They were also mentioned on March 28, 1408 and July 24, 1409. Dupont-Ferrier believes, however, that Poitou was not formally established as an *élection* until about 1412. He cites a document of December 16, 1412 which refers to the "clergy of the élection of Poitiers".[36] On March 25, 1416, Maître Jean Mérichon, royal secretary, was appointed as an *élu* in Poitou.[37] He was accompanied by

---

[33]   B. N., p.o. vol. 2855, Torsay, doss. 63,456, no. 11; *Ibid.*, Vol. 201, La Barre, no. 9.
[34]   Dupont-Ferrier, "De quelques problèmes", *Journal des Savants* (August-October, 1928), 355.
[35]   G. Dupont-Ferrier, "Essai sur la géographie administrative des élections financières en France de 1356 à 1790", *Annuaire-Bulletin de la Société de l'Histoire de France* (1929), LXVI, 295, hereafter cited as Dupont-Ferrier, "Essai sur la géographie administrative", *Ann. Bul. Soc. Hist. France.*
[36]   *Ibid.*
[37]   G. Dupont-Ferrier, *Etudes sur les institutions financières de la France à la*

the previously appointed *élus* of that province to their office and seated
at their side. A letter of April 10 of the same year from the *élus* of Poitou has survived.[38] There seems to be no further mention of them until
October 23, 1430.[39] After this latter date, references to them become
more numerous. An interesting document of May 25, 1433 definitely
indicates that there had been *élus* in Poitou for some time. The royal
advocate declares that:

in Poitou it was originally ordained that there be two *élus*; later, there was
a third. Thus, there were always three, and this was sufficient. Now Maître
Jean Colas claims to be the fourth *élu*.[40]

After 1430 the role of the *élus* in Poitou is fairly clear. Before 1430,
however, their activity remains shrouded in uncertainty. In fact, not a
single document discovered by the present writer that refers to taxes in
Poitou before this date made any mention of the *élus*. Generally, the
three estates voted the tax and specially appointed royal commissioners
apportioned and collected it.

Perhaps the role of the *élus* from their appearance in the province in
about 1403 until 1416 may be explained very simply. During this period
Poitou formed part of the apanage of John, duke of Berry. Each tax
voted by the estates of Poitou during these years was granted to the duke
and he appointed his own commissioners to collect it. The *élus*, being
royal officials, obviously had nothing to do with this. The king, however,
also levied royal taxes in the area for the conduct of the war. Charles
VI imposed such taxes arbitrarily without consulting either the Estates
General or local estates. Undoubtedly, the *élus* looked after the collection of these royal taxes.

Between 1416 and 1430 the present writer found no mention at all
of the *élus* in Poitou. In fact, it is interesting to note that in a detailed
work on the *élections* of France, in which he cites dozens of examples
for each *élection*, Dupont-Ferrier gives very few examples of *élus* or
élections during the 1420's for the part of France under French rule.[41]
Usually his examples skip from about 1418 to the 1430's. This gap can
be explained quite simply, however, by the fact that Dupont-Ferrier was

---

fin du moyen âge (Paris, 1930-32), I, 73, note 1, hereafter cited as Dupont-Ferrier,
Etudes sur les institutions financières.

[38] *Ibid.*, II, 247, note 699.
[39] B. N., ms. fr. 20,594, no. 25.
[40] Dupont-Ferrier, *Etudes sur les institutions financières*, I, 66, note 7.
[41] Dupont-Ferrier, "Essai sur la géographie administrative", *Ann. Soc. Hist.
France*, LXV and LXVI.

relying chiefly upon the registers of the Cour des Aides for his information and there is a gap in these registers between 1416 and 1427.[42] In
all probability the *élus* continued to function in Poitou during these
years, but a lack of information renders a detailed account of their activities impossible.[43]

After 1430 there is no shortage of information about the *élus* in
Poitou, and their role can be described with more assurance. For a few
years they seem to have shared with temporarily appointed royal commissioners the responsibility of apportioning and collecting taxes. However, the consent of the three estates of Poitou to royal taxes was still
sought for another five or six years. For example, royal letters of October
23, 1430 were addressed to the "elus sur le fait des aides" in Poitou
instructing them to impose a tax of 40,000 *livres tournois* plus 4500
livres for *frais*.[44] They state, however, that both principal and *frais* had
been granted by the three estates of Poitou. Also, royal letters of November 17, 1430 addressed to the *élus* and authorizing payment of 800
livres to the lord of Mareuil, to be paid from the same *frais*, reiterate
that this sum had been granted by the three estates.[45] The increasing
activity of the *élus* in Poitou is again indicated by royal letters of May
2, 1433 instructing them to impose a tax of 68,000 *livres tournois* as
that province's share of an *aide* granted the king by the Estates General.[46]
This time no mention is made of the estates of Poitou.

In August or September 1434 the estates of Poitou, the *élus*, and
the royal commissioners all participated in the levying of a tax. In August a joint assembly of the estates of Poitou, Saintonge, Anjou, and
Touraine voted a subsidy to the king. Royal letters of September 2
were addressed to both the *élus* and to the commissioners instructing
them to impose in Poitou that province's share of the tax.[47] Similarly,
royal letters of September 7 were addressed to the

---

[42]   Register Z 1a6 stops in 1416. Z 1a7 and Z 1a9 concern the *Cour des Comptes*
of Paris under English administration. Z 1a8 covers the period 1428-1434 for the
Cour des Aides established at Poitiers by Charles VII, leaving a gap from 1416 to
1427 for the part of France under French control. I am indebted to M. Robert
Favreau, archivist of the department of Maine-et-Loire for this information which
has forced me to change several opinions I expressed in *Mediaeval Studies*,
XXVI, 201-02 regarding the activity of the *élus* during these years.
[43]   M. Favreau assures me that he has found several references to *élus* in Poitou
between 1416 and 1430 in his own research.
[44]   B. N., ms. fr. 20,594, no. 25.
[45]   *Ibid.*, p.o. vol. 1849, Mareuil, doss, 42,690, no. 31.
[46]   A. N., K 63, no. 25. No other information is available about this alleged
assembly of the Estates General.
[47]   B. N., Collection Clairambault, 194, fol. 7691.

esleuz sur le fait des aides and to the commissioners entrusted with imposing in our *pays* of Poitou the *aide* that was granted to us at the assembly of the three estates held in this our town of Tours last August.[48]

The roll of *tailles* for Poitou, dated September 30, 1434, refers to this tax voted by the joint assembly of estates and declares that it was to be levied in Poitou by Maurice Claveurier, Simon Mourrault, Henri Blandin, and other "elus sur le fait desd. aides".[49]

In 1435 the *élus*, royal commissioners, and the estates of Poitou all participated in the levying of a tax. On July 8 the four royal commissioners wrote to the *élus sur le fait des aides* in Poitou.[50] By virtue of the powers granted them by royal letters of June 15, they ordered the *élus* to collect a tax of 61,500 *livres tournois*, which the estates of Poitou had granted the king for four years in lieu of indirect *aides*. They were instructed how and when to collect the tax. They were to turn over the amount collected to a receiver appointed by the king. In this case, then, the procedure is clear. The royal commissioners summoned the estates, the estates voted the tax, the commissioners then instructed the *élus* to collect it, specifying the procedure to be followed, the *élus* collected it and turned it over to a royal receiver.

This is the last time that the three estates of Poitou seem to have voted the royal tax, and this is the last occasion for many years on which the royal commissioners are mentioned in connection with the collection of a tax in Poitou. Henceforth the *élus* seem to have taken over completely the functions previously exercised chiefly by the estates and the commissioners. In January 1436 the *élus* were instructed to impose a tax of 9000 *livres tournois* in the province, plus an additional 2000 *livres* for *frais*.[51] In the same year, on some date prior to April 27, the *élus* were ordered to impose a sum of 2300 *livres tournois* over and above Poitou's share of a tax granted the king in February by the Estates General of Languedoil. This extra amount had been voted by the estates of Poitou to buy a wedding present for the dauphin [52] but there is nothing to indicate that the three estates of Poitou has been called upon to consent to the provinces' share of the main tax. In March 1438, the *élus* were ordered to raise Poitou's share of a tax which had been imposed on Languedoil by the king without the consent of the Estates

[48] A. N., K 63, no. 36.
[49] La Boutetière, "Rôle des tailles", *M. S. A. O.*, II, 499.
[50] B. N., ms. fr. 25,969, no. 956.
[51] *Ibid.*, ms. fr. 21,428, fol. 11.
[52] A. N., K 64, no. 11.

General.[53] In March 1442, the *élus* were instructed to impose a sum of 1650 *livres tournois* over and above the principal of the next tax to be imposed on Poitou.[54] This extra sum was to pay for a royal grant to Charles of Anjou. It does not appear that the consent of the estates of Poitou was sought on any of the above occasions. In short, all evidence seems to prove that, after about 1436, the *élus* handled the entire process of raising and collecting taxes in Poitou without the participation of the estates or of royal commissioners.

From the above, it is clear that Thomas's assertion that the appearance of *élus* in a province indicates the decline and decadence of the provincial estates [55] cannot be accepted as a valid generalization without some qualifications. It is probably true for regions where *élus* appeared for the first time under Charles VII, as in the provinces which Thomas was studying. In areas like Poitou, however, where they were introduced earlier, the story was somewhat different. During the reign of Charles VI and the early part of the reign of Charles VII the presence of royal *élus* in Poitou did not seem to restrict noticeably the activities of the provincial estates. From about 1418 to about 1430 the role of the *élus* in Poitou cannot be described in detail due to a shortage of information. By 1430 at least they were sharing with the three estates and the royal commissioners in the levying of taxes. Then, about 1435, the *élus* took over completely the functions formerly exercised chiefly by these two latter groups.

One important point remains to be discussed concerning the financial activities of the three estates of Poitou. This is the fundamental question of why they ceased to consent to royal taxes in about 1435. There are two aspects of this question. In the first place, why did the king cease to summon them to vote taxes? In the second place, why did the people accept this policy without any apparent protest?

The first part of the question appears to be the simpler of the two to answer. When the king began to impose taxes arbitrarily without summoning the Estates General or the provincial estates, he was merely following a policy of extending royal authority that had been going on, with some interruptions, for more than two and a half centuries. As far back as the reign of Philip Augustus, royal advisors and officials had been consistently working to increase the power of the monarch. During the years following the disaster of Agincourt, when half of the country

[53] B. N., ms. fr. 21,428, fol. 12, and 23,909, fol. 1.
[54] A. N., K 67, no. 10.
[55] Thomas, *Les Etats provinciaux*, p. 167.

was in the hands of the English, the royal government was in no position to continue this policy. During the 1430's and 1440's, however, when the tide of battle turned steadily in favor of the French, the position of the king of France became steadily stronger. In 1435 the decisive alliance with Burgundy was concluded, and in 1436 Paris was recaptured. Charles VII and his capable advisors then turned to the traditional policy of extending the authority of the royal government.[56] One aspect of this policy was the imposing of taxes in many parts of France without the consent of the Estates General or of provincial estates.

It is interesting to note that the three estates of Poitou ceased to vote royal taxes at approximately the same time as the Estates General lost this right. This is about fifteen or sixteen years earlier than the estates of Auvergne, Limousin, and La Marche ceased to consent to taxes. Perhaps the reason for this is that Poitou was one of the strongest centers of royal power throughout the entire reign of Charles VII. It is possible that the king felt strong enough to dispense with the consent of the local estates to taxation in Poitou earlier than in Auvergne, Limousin, and La Marche where his authority was slightly less secure.

The question of why the people of France accepted with little or no protest the royal policy of imposing taxes without the consent of the estates is somewhat more difficult to answer. A number of factors probably contributed to this acceptance.

In the first place, it should be remembered that, by the reign of Charles VII, both the clergy and the nobles were exempt from regular royal taxes.[57] Hence, members of the first two estates saw no special advantage in the provincial estates being called upon to consent to taxa-

[56] The nature of this extension of royal authority should not be misunderstood. It is merely relative to the weak position to which the French monarchy had sunk between 1415 and 1429, and we are still far from the absolute monarchy of Louis XIV. In fact, the French monarchy during the last half of the fifteenth century might be described as popular and consultative in nature rather than absolute. Nevertheless, many of the seeds of royal absolutism were being sown.

[57] The question of special taxes imposed upon the clergy cannot be discussed in detail in this work. Such taxes, or *décimes*, were levied occasionally by the king ever since the twelfth century. Until the mid-sixteenth century, special papal approval was usually sought. When these *décimes* became regular after 1561, they were consented to by regular assemblies of the clergy of France. Assemblies were then held of the clergy of each diocese to consent to their share and apportion it. See Doucet, II, 854. Numerous examples of such assemblies in the three dioceses composing Poitou could be cited during the years following 1561. See A. D. Vienne, G 398-403, and Collection Dom Fonteneau, XIV, 739. Hence, in the case of these special taxes imposed upon the clergy, the principle of consent to taxation was preserved.

tion. In fact, they were probably relieved when they were freed from the expense and trouble of attending frequent assemblies for this purpose. As far as the third estate is concerned, only the larger towns were represented at assemblies of estates during the reign of Charles VII. The peasants and inhabitants of lesser towns had never been represented in these assemblies and were in no way affected when the estates ceased to vote taxes. Hence, the only people who might have had any cause for complaint were the inhabitants of the principal towns and it is possible that many of them felt that they might be able to gain better terms by negotiating directly with the king.

In Poitou, not more than seven or eight towns were represented at assemblies of the provincial estates during the reign of Charles VII. Of these, the town of Poitiers played the dominant role and hence was the most affected when the king ceased to summon the three estates of the province to consent to taxation. Let us examine briefly taxes imposed on Poitiers from about 1435 down through the reign of Louis XII to see if the town suffered greatly from this change in royal policy.

During the last twenty-six years of the reign of Charles VII, Poitiers seems to have paid its share of the taxes imposed on Poitou without any negotiation. The town's portion was fixed by the royal *élus*. Two examples from other parts of the province show that it was possible to secure tax reductions by direct negotiation with the king, however. On November 21, 1440, the town of Saint-Maixent was granted a reduction in its share of the *taille*.[58] On March 16, 1459, the inhabitants of Lower Poitou were granted an exemption from taxes.[59]

During the reign of Louis XI, Poitiers seems to have fared better by direct negotiation with the king than it might have expected to through the medium of the estates. In fact, it obtained complete exemption from all regular *tailles*, which were imposed elsewhere in Poitou annually and without consent.[60] The town was subject to quite a few special taxes, however, and in such cases, its consent does not seem to have been sought. For example, in 1469 the town was taxed 5000 *livres* to pay for the expense of transferring the Parlement from Bordeaux to Poitiers.[61] In 1472 it was taxed 2000 *livres* for the maintenance of the army.[62]

---

[58]   G. du Fresne de Beaucourt, *Histoire de Charles VII* (Paris, 1881-91), III, 461, hereafter cited as Beaucourt.
[59]   *Ibid.*, VI, 378. Beaucourt does not specify exactly what types of taxes were covered by this exemption.
[60]   Henri Sée, *Louis XI et les villes* (Paris, 1891), p. 127.
[61]   *Ibid.*, p. 128.
[62]   *Ibid.*

When Louis XI demanded a special tax of 4000 *livres* in 1473, the town attempted to negotiate but was unsuccessful.[63] It protested that it was impoverished, sent 2000 *livres*, and begged to be excused from the remainder. The king's heart was in no way melted by this plea and the town was ordered to pay a further 1000 *livres* within three days. In September 1475 Louis XI ordered a tax of 2000 *livres* to be imposed on all inhabitants of Poitiers exempt or non-exempt.[64] It was stated that this was for one time only and would not prejudice their privileges and exemptions. The town did escape several other taxes imposed by Louis XI on Poitou, however. In November 1472 the king imposed a tax of 64,356 *livres* on Poitou for the payment of one hundred and seventy-three lances.[65] The town of Poitiers was exempt from this subsidy. In April 1479 Louis XI levied a tax in Poitou for the expenses of the royal artillery.[66] Once again Poitiers was not required to contribute.

Charles VIII, on occasion, also imposed special taxes on the town of Poitiers and there is nothing to indicate that he sought the consent of the inhabitants. For example, in February 1492 he sent two commissioners to Poitiers to levy a tax of 9000 *livres tournois* to pay three hundred foot soldiers for six months.[67] An undated letter from Louis XII to the mayor and *échevins* of Poitiers shows that the king still, on occasion, sought the consent of the town for a particular tax, however.[68] The letter states that the king had sent commissioners to the town to ask the inhabitants to grant him a tax of 5000 *livres tournois* to help meet his great expenses for the defense of the kingdom. After having heard their complaints, however, the commissioners had agreed to reduce this sum to 4000 *livres*. This case proves two interesting facts. In the first place, it shows that the principle of consent to taxation was still alive. In the second place, it shows that the town of Poitiers could still, on occasion, obtain by direct negotiation a reduction in the amount of a tax that the king sought to impose.

There is also another factor that may explain in part why there was no serious protest in Poitou, or elsewhere, when the king of France

---

[63] *Ibid.*, pp. 128-29.
[64] A. C. Poitiers, I, 11.
[65] Sée, *Louis XI et les villes*, p. 155, note 3.
[66] B. N., ms. fr. 12,041, published in part by L. de la Boutetière, "Un impôt de guerre en 1479", *Annuaire Départemental de la Société d'Emulation de la Vendée*, ser. 2, IX (1878-79), 499.
[67] A. C. Poitiers, I, 12 bis.
[68] B. N., ms. fr. 5,501, fol. 82.

began to impose taxes without the consent of the estates. As we have seen, Charles VII introduced a new tax in 1445 known as the *taille des gens de querre*. For the next six years he imposed this in addition to the regular *taille*. By 1451 the war with the English was practically over. Consequently, the king's need for money was greatly diminished. Therefore, Charles VII abolished the regular *taille* and reduced the amount of the *taille des gens de guerre*. This substantial reduction in taxes undoubtedly made those groups of the French people whom this affected more willing to accept taxation without the consent of the estates.

Let us sum up briefly the extent to which the above factors explain the apparent lack of protest in Poitou when the king ceased to summon the three estates of the province to vote taxes. As we have seen, the only people who were affected were the inhabitants of seven or eight principal towns and especially those of Poitiers. Between 1435 and 1451 it is very likely that there was some discontent over the new royal policy. It may have been softened somewhat by patriotic enthusiasm for the war effort and by a growing respect for the monarchy. The substantial tax reduction in 1451 almost certainly made this policy more acceptable. Then, during the reign of Louis XI, when taxes in France were very high, the town of Poitiers actually fared better by direct negotiation with the king than it could have expected to through the medium of the estates. During the reign of Louis XII, Poitiers was called upon, on at least one occasion, to consent to a royal tax and was actually able to secure a reduction in the amount demanded. Hence, it is apparent that those in Poitou who were the most directly affected when the king began to impose taxes without the consent of the three estates did not suffer appreciably by the change in policy. Perhaps, then, the lack of protest when the estates of Poitou was no longer summoned to vote taxes is not as surprising as it might appear.[69]

B. ADVISORY

Several of the activities of the three estates of Poitou might be described as advisory in nature. As seen when discussing origins, this function of the estates seems to stem directly from the feudal obligation of the vassal to give advice (*consilium*) to his lord when called upon to do so. Like its financial functions, the advisory activity of the estates of Poitou was confined to the years prior to 1470.

[69] It should be noted, however, that the demand of the Estates General of 1484, that they be summoned to consent to all taxes, shows that the royal policy of imposing taxes arbitrarily was by no means accepted with universal enthusiasm.

John, duke of Berry, summoned the three estates of Poitou to give him advice on several occasions during the period when the province formed part of his apanage. For example, he assembled them in November 1412, and again on December 22, 1412, to advise him concerning negotiations which he was conducting with the English for the withdrawal of their troops in Poitou. He summoned them again in February 1413 to advise him on certain matters concerning the welfare of the province.

On at least three occasions, assemblies of one or more of the estates of Poitou were held to deliberate and give advice on the specific problem of the pillaging of the soldiers. In December 1425 the three estates of Poitou met at Saint-Maixent with the estates of Saintonge. They deliberated regarding the pillaging and disorders of lawless bands of soldiers. On March 20, 1428 an assembly of the barons of Poitou met at Niort. They had been summoned by the king to meet with the sire de Gaucourt, seneschal of Poitou, to find means of putting an end to the soldiers' pillaging. They do not seem to have accomplished very much. In August 1440, the three estates of Poitou met at Niort to discuss a way to stop the pillaging and depredations of various partisans of the Praguerie, notably Jean de la Roche and the duke of Alençon. This meeting led to a royal decision of September 18, 1440, ordering the use of a tax of 11,500 *livres*, which was to be levied in Poitou, to bring about the evacuation of the region by these lawless bands.[70]

On at least one occasion, the three estates of Poitou met to discuss negotiations with a warlike noble. In November 1416, they were summoned by the dauphin Charles, probably acting as count of Poitou, regarding negotiations with Jean L'Archevêque, sire de Parthenay. The latter, an adherent of the duke of Burgundy, had been carrying on a bloody struggle in Poitou with the followers of Richemont, the future constable.[71] The dauphin, who had recently become count of Poitou following the death of his elder brother, John, was seeking to restore order. The negotiations failed and the sire de Parthenay continued his pillaging. In fact, the delegates from Poitiers had to return home by a round-about route to avoid attack.[72]

It is interesting to note that, even though the three estates of Poitou were no longer summoned to give advice after the early years of the reign of Louis XI, more restricted assemblies were sometimes held by

[70]   Beaucourt, III, 413.
[71]   Bélisaire Ledain, *La Gâtine historique et monumentale* (Paris, 1876), p. 196.
[72]   A. C. Poitiers, J 546.

royal officials for this purpose. For example, on August 12, 1574, the officers of justice, *élus*, mayors, *échevins*, and principal inhabitants of the towns of Niort, Fontenay-le-Comte, and Saint-Maixent assembled in Niort.[73] They were summoned by the count of Le Lude, as governor of Poitou, acting in accordance with the instructions of the duke of Montpensier, royal lieutenant in Brittany, Poitou, Saintonge, and Angoumois. They offered suggestions for prosecuting the war against the Protestants in the area and complained about the actions of the soldiers. They requested that, if further subsidies were necessary, the inhabitants of the provinces of that area be allowed to assemble to discuss them.

The duke of Montpensier was probably referring to this same assembly when he wrote to the officers of justice, *élus*, mayors, and *échevins* of Poitiers on September 3, 1574.[74] He stated that, because he had been having difficulty in getting sufficient supplies for the army, he had summoned the principal inhabitants of certain towns to receive their suggestions. They had proposed that a certain sire de la Barberye be paid to provide the necessary provisions. The *chevaliers*, captains, and council of the army had then decided how the sum of money which would be required would be apportioned in Poitou, Saintonge and Angoulême. The duke informed the above town officials that the share for the *élection* of Poitiers had been fixed at 7600 *livres*. It is apparent that the delegates present at the assembly at Niort had not been consulted about the amount of this tax or its apportionment. The fact that they had been summoned to give advice on other related matters is of interest, however.

C. PRESENTING GRIEVANCES AND MAKING REQUESTS

Presenting grievances and making requests were important functions of the three estates of Poitou throughout the entire period of their existence. Sometimes they merely took advantage of the opportunity when they had been assembled for other reasons but, on some occasions in the mid-fifteenth century, they actually took the initiative, met of their own volition, and sent a deputation to the king bearing their grievances.[75] After the reign of Louis XI, however, the estates of Poitou always obtained special royal permission before holding an assembly to discuss presenting grievances or making requests to the king.

[73]   *A. H. P.*, XX, 368-80.
[74]   *Ibid.*, XXVII, 177-78.
[75]   The preparation by the estates of Poitou of lists of grievances to be presented at meetings of the Estates General will be discussed in section F. of this chapter.

Many of the complaints sent to the king by the estates of Poitou concerned the salt tax. While the well-known and unpopular *gabelle* became general throughout most of France during the last half of the fourteenth century, some salt producing provinces, such as Poitou, were subject instead to another tax known as the *quart du sel*. In these provinces, merchants took their salt to specially designated towns. There the value of the salt was settled by discussion between the merchant and a special royal official. The latter then collected, to the profit of the government, a tax equal to one quarter of the agreed price plus an additional sum to cover the wages of the personnel of his office. The merchant was then given a certificate which allowed him to sell his salt at the agreed price. The twenty-five percent tax had to be paid again each time the salt was resold.

King John and John, duke of Berry, had both considered establishing the *gabelle* in Poitou but, after careful investigation, had decided against it.[76] In 1383 Charles VI raised the tax to one half the price of the salt. The protests were so vehement and so many salt workers left Poitou, that the *quart* was soon reestablished. In 1445 Charles VII again began to consider extending the *gabelle* to Poitou and Saintonge in order to increase his revenues. This led to a series of protests from the inhabitants of the area and to at least one assembly of the three estates of Poitou.

In July 1445 the town of Poitiers sent a petition to the king asking him not to impose the *gabelle* in Poitou.[77] It apparently went unheeded and on October 26, 1446, the town council of Poitiers decided to send another delegation.[78] In order to give their protest more weight, they convoked the clergy, nobles, and townsmen of the province to meet on November 10 and add their remonstrances.

Four years later the matter was still pending. Although the king had taken no definite action, he was still thinking of extending the *gabelle* to Poitou. Accordingly, the town of Poitiers decided to take further action and in late 1450, sent two delegates to contact the nobles, good towns and clergy of the province to obtain their arguments against the imposition of this tax. Whether the three estates of Poitou were assembled or whether these two delegates travelled throughout the prov-

---

[76] *Mémoires présentés au roi Charles VII par les délégués de la ville de Poitiers pour le détourner d'établir la gabelle en Poitou et en Saintonge*, ed. B. Ledain, *A. H. P.*, II, 253-84, hereafter cited as *Mémoires présentés au roi Charles VII, A. H. P.*, II.

[77] *Ibid.*, 254.

[78] Régistres de Poitiers, reg. 3, fol. 81.

ince instead, cannot be determined. On January 3, 1451 they presented their report to the town council of Poitiers.[79] They reported that the clergy, nobles, and good towns of the province were willing to add their protests against the imposition of the *gabelle* to a petition which was to be sent to the king. Two members of the town council were then appointed to incorporate the various arguments which they had received against the imposition of the *gabelle* into a petition.[80] It was taken to Tours and presented to the king by a deputation from the town of Poitiers.[81] That the king was temporarily dissuaded from imposing the *gabelle* is indicated by the fact that in 1451, and again in March 1452, he issued instructions about the manner in which the *quart* was to be levied in Poitou and Saintonge.[82] The matter was still not settled permanently, however, and a new delegation was sent to the king in February 1454.[83] This time it was completely successful. The *gabelle* was not established and the less onerous *quart* was retained.

Nearly a century elapsed before the estates of Poitou again concerned itself with salt taxes. By then, however, changes in royal policy had made the matter an issue once again. Between the years 1549 and 1553, the three estates of Poitou met at least five times, and probably oftener, to discuss replacing the existing form of salt tax. Some of these meetings were held jointly with the estates of certain adjoining provinces which were also concerned. A brief explanation of the royal policy with regard to salt taxes in western and southwestern France during the first half of the sixteenth century is necessary for a proper understanding of these assemblies of estates.[84]

While most of France was subject to the *gabelle* during the early years of the sixteenth century, some provinces continued to be exempt from it and paid only the less burdensome *quart du sel*. Included in this latter group were Guyenne, Saintonge, Aunis, Angoumois, Poitou, Périgord, Limousin and La Marche. In 1537 the *quart* was increased to a *quart* and *demi-quart*, which meant that the merchant paid a tax equal to three-eights of the value of the salt. On June 1, 1541 an edict was passed doing away with the *quart* and *demi-quart* and imposing a universal tax of 44 *livres* per *muid* on salt, to be levied at the salt marshes.

[79] *Ibid.*, reg. 4, fol. 19.
[80] In all probability, the document published by Ledain is the petition which they prepared. *Mémoires présentés au Roi Charles VII, A. H. P.*, II, 253-84.
[81] A. C. Poitiers, J 1117 and 1118.
[82] Beaucourt, V, 340-41.
[83] *Mémoires présentés au roi Charles VII, A. H. P.*, II, 255-56.
[84] For more detail on this and on the subsequent revolts over the *gabelle*, see

This was never enforced and was replaced by a law of April 7, 1542, reducing the tax to 24 *livres* per *muid*, but extending it to include salt destined for export and for the fishing industry. This was ruinous to the salt producing regions and revolts occurred in Saintonge and Aunis. The law was revoked on May 1, 1543, and the *quart et demi-quart* was re-established. Finally, however, the royal government, constantly in need of money, extended the *gabelle* to the entire kingdom by Ordonnances of July 1, and December 6, 1544. As it took some time to establish the salt warehouses, revolts did not break out immediately. An uprising occurred in Saintonge in 1546 and a more serious revolt broke out in Angoumois, Saintonge and Guyenne in 1548.[85]

The revolt threatened to spread to Poitou. The town of Poitiers, loyal to the king, took measures to defend itself and no disturbances occurred.[86] Two royal armies under constable Montmorency and the duke of Aumale put down the insurrection in Guyenne, Angoumois and Saintonge in September 1548. They stopped in Poitiers on their way home and were greeted by the lieutenant-general of Poitou, François Doyneau. After having congratulated them on their victory, he pointed out the unpopularity of the *gabelle* and asked them to explain to the king that the old tax of the *quart* and the *demi-quart* would prove to be just as profitable in the long run and would be much less unpopular. Montmorency and d'Aumale promised to convey this message to the king and suggested that the town send envoys to the royal court to request that the *gabelle* be abolished in return for a cash grant by the provinces concerned.

Soon after, the town council of Poitiers met and elected two deputies to go to the royal court as Montmorency and d'Aumale had suggested.[87] Two or three months later, these two deputies were received by the king in a private audience. They declared that the *gabelle* was ruinous and requested its repeal in return for a cash payment. The king received their proposal favourably and appointed four royal commissioners [88] with instructions to assemble in Poitiers the estates of Poitou, Châtellerault, Saintonge, the town and *gouvernement* of La Rochelle, Angoumois, Haut

---

Commandant Déruelle, "La révolte de la gabelle en Angoumois et en Saintonge (1548-1549), *Bulletin de la Société des Archives Historiques, Revue de la Saintonge et de l'Aunis*, XXVII (Saintes, 1907), 91 and following, hereafter cited as Déruelle, "La révolte de la gabelle."

[85] Jean Bouchet, *Les Annales d'Aquitaine* (Poitiers, 1644), pp. 564-66, hereafter cited as Bouchet.

[86] *Ibid.*, p. 567.

[87] Bouchet himself attended this meeting as one of the bourgeois of Poitiers.

[88] Déruelle, "La révolte de la gabelle", pp. 192-93, only names three commissioners.

and Bas Limousin, Haute and Basse Marche and Périgord. At this meeting, the royal commissioners were to hear the offers made by the estates for the repeal of the *gabelle*.

Before this assembly in Poitiers took place, it is possible that delegates from Poitou attended some kind of assembly of estates at Tarbes on April 28, 1549, summoned by Anthony of Bourbon, King of Navarre, acting as lieutenant-governor of Guyenne. Whether this had anything to do with the *gabelle* cannot be established definitely but it is likely that it did. A letter from the king of Navarre, dated March 25, 1549, and addressed to the seneschal and his lieutenants, the *élus* and other royal officers, the mayors and *jurats* of the *sénéchaussée* of Poitou, provides the only information available. It states that he has received their complaints about taxes and invites two of them, or any others who might be chosen by the people of the province, to attend at Tarbes on Quasimodo (April 28) an assembly of deputies from all of the provinces and *sénéchaussées* of his jurisdiction. At this meeting he would make known his proposals. If this assembly was ever held, its precise nature and its results cannot be determined.

The efforts of the two deputies from Poitiers who attended the royal court, as described above, did bear direct fruit, however. As he had promised by letters patent of May 5, the king authorized the estates of the provinces concerned to assemble in Poitiers on July 11.[89] The meeting began on the morning of the appointed day. The estates offered the king 450,000 *livres* (200,000 *écus*) if he would abolish the *gabelle* and restore the *quart* and *demi-quart*. They also chose six deputies to go to the royal court and complete the arrangements.[90]

On August 12 these delegates appeared before the court at Amiens and Abbéville.[91] Negotiations were delayed by the unwillingness of the nobles to contribute in spite of their earlier promise to do so. They finally agreed to pay their share and by letters patent of September 1549, Henry II abolished the *gabelle* in Poitou, Châtellerault, Saintonge, the *gouvernement* of La Rochelle, Angoumois, Haut and Bas Limousin, Haute and Basse Marche, and Périgord, and reestablished the *quart* and *demi-quart*.[92] The king was to receive the 450,000 *livres* offered him by the estates of these provinces. In addition, he stipulated that the receivers

---

[89] Régistres de Poitiers, reg. 30, July 6, 1549.
[90] *Documents inédits pour servir à l'histoire du Poitou, publiés par la Société des Antiquaires de l'Ouest* (Poitiers, 1876), pp. 157-58, hereafter cited as *Documents inédits pour l'histoire du Poitou.*
[91] Déruelle, "La révolte de la gabelle", p. 193.
[92] Bouchet, p. 574; A. C. Poitiers, C 30.

of the salt warehouses who had purchased their offices, must be reimbursed.[93] This would cost an estimated 25,000 *livres*. The estates of the various provinces were granted the right either to farm out the collection of the *quart et demi-quart* or have it collected by receivers whom they would choose. The king reserved the right, however, to appoint his own collectors at any time if he so desired. If it was found that the annual amount collected did not amount to at least 80,000 *livres tournois*, after the expenses of collection had been deducted, the difference would be collected from the provinces in any way the king saw fit. If in any one year the amount exceeded the 80,000 *livres tournois*, the excess could be counted for the next year, however. If these conditions were met for three years beginning on January 1, 1550, the date on which the abolition of the *gabelle* was to be effective, the *quart et demi-quart* would be levied thereafter with no strings attached.[94]

Early in October 1549, the king issued letters patent authorizing the seneschal of Poitou or his lieutenant to assemble in Poitiers the estates of the provinces concerned so that the 450,000 *livres*, plus the additional 25,000 *livres*, could be apportioned among them.[95] They met in Poitiers some time during November (after November 11), and the tax was apportioned among the various provinces. The third estate was to pay 2/3 of the sum and the first and second estates were to pay 1/6 each.[96]

In addition to this joint assembly with the estates of neighbouring provinces, several documents indicate that the estates of Poitou also met alone in Poitiers on November 18, 1549. Letters patent from Henry II, dated October 10, instructed François Doyneau, lieutenant-general of Poitou, to contact the bishops of the three dioceses of Poitou, the principal nobles, and the third estate regarding the apportioning of the tax.[97] This was to be settled by the end of November. These letters patent stated precisely the share of the clergy of each of the three dioceses of Poitiers, Luçon, and Maillezais, even breaking it down into their share of the main tax and their share of the 25,000 *livres* for the repayment of the officeholders of the *gabelle*.[98] It was stipulated that the clergy were to pay their share by January 1, 1550. The share of the principal tax

[93] Bouchet, p. 575; *Archives historiques de la ville de Fontenay-le-Comte réunies et mises en ordre par Benjamin Fillon avec la collaboration d'A. Bitton*, II, 185; Collection de Dom Fonteneau, II, 425.
[94] Bouchet, pp. 575-76.
[95] *Ibid.*, p. 577.
[96] Antoine Thibaudeau, *Histoire du Poitou* (Niort, 1839), II, 231.
[97] Régistres de Poitiers, reg. 31, November 5, 1549.
[98] Collection de Dom Fonteneau, II, 425 and 428.

was to be paid to the royal receivers in Poitiers while the share of the extra 25,000 *livres* was to be paid to whomever the estates had commissioned for this purpose. The estates of Poitou met at Poitiers on November 18, and ordained that within a week it must receive a statement of the names and revenues of all the nobles exempt from the *taille* so that they could proceed with the task of fixing their share of the tax.[99] It probably met again when it received this information.

A legal dispute which arose between the estates of the different provinces which had obtained the abolition of the *gabelle* gave rise to at least one more assembly involving the estates of Poitou. The deputies of Périgord and Bas Limousin claimed that the *quart* and *demi-quart* should be paid once only on the marshes or at the mouths of the rivers on any salt entering these provinces. Then the salt could be sold anywhere in the two provinces without anything further being paid on its sale, resale or exchange. The deputies of the other provinces which had obtained the abolition of the *gabelle* contested this claim and the case was brought before the royal privy council. The estates of Poitou, Saintonge, the *gouvernement* of La Rochelle, Angoumois, Haut Limousin, and Haute and Basse Marche met in Poitiers in November 1549, regarding this case and chose their legal representatives. They selected two lawyers to defend their interests before the privy council. The latter body was examining the matter during April, May and June 1550.[100] The case was still not settled by December 1, 1552. On this date, the estates of Périgord met at Sarlat and agreed that their delegates would continue to pursue the case before the king and his privy council.[101] It is more than likely that the estates of Poitou and of the other provinces involved met several times between November 1549 and the early part of 1553 concerning this dispute.[102] There is no record of the royal decision. In any case, the events of 1553 put an end to the issue under dispute, as will be seen below.

[99] A. C. Poitiers, C 30. This document could conceivably refer to the joint meeting in November described above, but the wording gives the impression that on this occasion the estates of Poitou was meeting alone.

[100] *Ibid.*, C 31. Also, Manuscrits de la Bibliothèque de Poitiers, 385 (36), pp. 355-56.

[101] L. de Cardenal, "Catalogue des assemblées des Etats du Périgord de 1378 à 1651", *Bulletin Philologique et Historique du Comité des Travaux Historiques et Scientifiques* (1938-39), p. 255, hereafter cited as Cardenal, "Catalogue des assemblées des Etats de Périgord."

[102] An assembly at Poitiers in 1550, at which deputies from Poitou and Guyenne were present, was probably for this purpose. *Archives Historiques du Département de la Gironde*, XXVIII (1893), 49. It is possible that Guyenne was also represented at the other assemblies of the previous year.

By 1553, the people of the provinces which had secured the abolition of the *gabelle* found even the *quart* and *demi-quart* insupportable.
They complained particularly of the money wasted paying the numerous
royal officials charged with collecting this tax and requested the king
to replace it with a straight cash payment.[103] He appointed three royal
commissioners to go to Saintes and meet with the mayors, *échevins* and
officials of the principal towns of the region.[104] Two delegates attended
from Poitiers.[105] These various town officials were instructed at this
meeting to assemble the three estates of their respective provinces to
discuss the offer to be made to the king for the repeal of the *quart* and
demi-quart.[106] At these meetings, they were also to elect deputies to attend a general assembly of the estates of all of the provinces concerned
in Poitiers on October 1. At this general assembly they would present
their offer to the royal officials. The precise date of the meeting in
Saintes cannot be determined. It probably took place late in August
and certainly before September 4.

The three estates of Poitou met in Poitiers on September 25 to discuss the offer to be made to the king and to elect deputies to attend the
general assembly on October 1. Then, on the latter date, the estates of
Poitou, Saintonge, the town and *gouvernement* of La Rochelle, Angoumois, Haut and Bas Limousin, Haute and Basse Marche, Périgord and
Guyenne met together in Poitiers to present their offer to the royal commissioners. Then delegates from the estates went to the royal court where
they were received on November 4, and their offer officially accepted.[107]

By letters of December 1553, Henry II abolished the *quart* and *demi-
quart* in Poitou, Saintonge, the town and *gouvernement* of La Rochelle,
Angoumois, Haut and Bas Limousin, Haute and Basse Marche, Périgord, and Guyenne in return for a payment of 1,195,000 *livres*.[108] This
was to be paid in two equal installments, the first due on March 1, 1554
and the second due on June 1, 1554. The third estate was to pay two
thirds of the total, or 796,000 *livres tournois*. The other third would be
split equally between the nobles and clergy, meaning that each would
pay 199,000 *livres*. The cost of collection was to be paid by the estates

[103] Collection de Dom Fonteneau, XXVII, ter., 141.
[104] *Ibid.*, also A. C. Poitiers, C 33. This meeting at Saintes was not an assembly
of estates, as Ledain believed; B. Ledain, "Les Maires de Poitiers", *M. S. A. O.*,
LX (1897), 549-50, hereafter cited as Ledain, "Maires de Poitiers."
[105] Régistres de Poitiers, reg. 32, September 21, 1553.
[106] Collection de Dom Fonteneau, XXVII, ter., 141; A. C. Poitiers, C 33.
[107] Collection de Dom Fonteneau, XXVII, ter., 141; Régistres de Poitiers, reg.
32, October 16, 1553.
[108] A. C. Poitiers, C 33; Collection de Dom Fonteneau, XXVII, ter., 141.

and the extra money necessary for this would be collected by men whom they would appoint themselves. This time they were not required to reimburse the "farmers" of the *quart* and *demi-quart*. It was declared unlawful to transport salt from those provinces where this tax was abolished into those where the *gabelle* was enforced. The king promised not to impose any salt taxes in future in the provinces in question. Other documents show the precise share of the 1,194,000 *livres* to be paid by the clergy of the three dioceses included in Poitou.[109] The royal letters patent abolishing the *quart et demi-quart* were registered in the Cour des Aides on January 17, 1554.[110] At this time it was stipulated that, within six months, the three estates of each province must send a detailed statement to the Cour des Aides of the expenses involved in collecting their share of the tax. Hence, it is possible that the estates of Poitou met once again during the first half of 1554 to prepare this statement.

It is apparent then that between the summer of 1549 and the early part of 1554 the estates of Poitou met frequently, sometimes alone and sometimes with the estates of other provinces, to discuss the salt taxes and make offers to the king for their repeal. Indeed, during this four or five year period, the estates of Poitou and of the neighbouring provinces show a continuity of action usually associated only with the *pays d'états* by the sixteenth century.

Nearly a century later, efforts to reestablish the *gabelle* in Poitou led to a protest being sent to the king. The somewhat fragmentary information available has led one historian to believe that the three estates of the province met to prepare this protest.[111] Let us examine this possibility.

During the year 1651, the farmers of the *gabelle* had been attempting to reestablish their offices in Lower Poitou.[112] In a meeting of the town council of Poitiers on July 31, it was decided that a petition would be sent to the king regarding the complaints of various communities and parishes of Lower Poitou that the *gabelle* was being imposed upon them in spite of exemptions granted by previous kings.[113] One of the *échevins* had drawn up this petition and read it to those present at the meeting. They decided to send it to another *échevin* who happened to be in Paris, so that he could present it to the king. The result was an order from the royal council, dated September 4, stating that the king had received the

---

109 *Ibid.*, II, 447; A. D. Vienne, G 395.
110 Collection de Dom Fonteneau, XXVII, ter., 141.
111 Thibaudeau, *Histoire de Poitou*, II, 236.
112 Régistres de Poitiers, reg. 103, July 31 and September 25, 1651.
113 *Ibid.*, July 31, 1651.

remonstrances of the "deputies of the nobles of Poitou, the towns and communities of Poitiers, Fontenay-le-Comte, Thouars, and others." [114] The council decreed that all offices of the *gabelle* which had been established in Poitou be closed and that the transport of salt from the Poitevin marshes be free of charge provided that it was consumed within the province. This decree was officially registered on September 15, 1651.[115]

It is difficult to determine from the above information what sort of assembly, if any, was held in Poitou to prepare this petition. The remonstrances were apparently sent to the king in August and the royal reply was dated September 4. The estates of Poitou met on July 3 to elect deputies to an assembly of the Estates General to be held at Tours on September 8.[116] The deputies actually went to Tours and were not informed of the postponement of the assembly until September 11. In other words, at the time the petition regarding the salt tax was made to the king, it was still believed that the Estates General would meet. If it was prepared at the assembly of the estates of Poitou on July 3, or if they held another assembly later for this specific purpose, why was it not taken to Tours by their deputies to be presented at the meeting of the Estates General along with the other grievances of the province? The answer is not apparent. There are two conclusions that appear most likely. The first is that the petition formed part of the *cahiers* of the nobles and third estate of Poitou prepared at their assembly of July 3, and for some reason which cannot be determined, it was decided to present it directly to the king, before the assembly of the Estates General. The second is that it was not prepared at any assembly at all but was merely a petition arranged by correspondence between the town councils of several towns of Poitou to which a number of individual nobles added their names. In any case, it does not seem likely, in view of the circumstances, that a special assembly of the three estates of Poitou was held to prepare it.

Protests concerning salt taxes were by no means the only grievances presented to the king by the three estates of Poitou. During the fifteenth century, they made requests or sent petitions to the king about other matters on a number of occasions.

In June 1417, the delegates of the estates of Poitou complained to the dauphin Charles of the pillaging of the Bretons and Picards in garrison at Parthenay, Vouvent and Mervent. The Picards were follow-

---

[114] *Ibid.*, September 25, 1651.
[115] B. N., ms. fr., n.a. 10,018, fol. 54, no. 597.
[116] See Appendix A, Catalogue of Assemblies.

ers of the sire de Parthenay; the Bretons were supporters of Richemont. It will be recalled that these two factions were fighting bitterly in Poitou.

In May 1418, the estates of Poitou, Saintonge, Limousin, Périgord, Angoumois, and La Marche met together, probably at Limoges, and sent a request to the dauphin asking that two royal commissioners be sent to Poitou. The purpose of this commission cannot be ascertained but the request was granted.

Of special interest are several occasions in the mid-fifteenth century when the town council of Poitiers took the initiative and assembled the estates of the province to discuss presenting grievances to the king. This occurred, for example, in November 1447. This assembly chose a delegation consisting of five representatives of the town council of Poitiers, two representatives of the other towns of the province and two representatives of the nobles, to present their grievances to the king.[117] The delegation appeared before the king at Vincennes and complained of ills of all kinds which the province had suffered from brigandage. They stressed the resulting poverty and begged for a reduction in the *taille*. The king greeted them favourably, promised tax reductions and expressed the affection he had always felt for Poitou.

On August 9, 1461, the three estates of Poitou met again at the instigation of the town council of Poitiers. Their purpose was to choose a delegation to send to the new king, Louis XI, to seek the abolition of the *aides*. They were assembled again for the same purpose in September by the sire de Belleville, royal commissioner charged with receiving oaths of loyalty to the new king in Poitou. They decided to send a deputation to the king with instructions to do everything possible to obtain the abolition of the *aides*. Four delegates left for Tours on October 26 and remained there until December 9.[118] The outcome of their mission is not known.

Finally in August 1466, the estates of Poitou once again sent a list of grievances to the king. On July 25, the king had written to the town council and clergy of Poitiers asking them to send their written observations on abuses in the administration of finance and justice and on the perennial problem of the pillaging of soldiers, to royal commissioners in Etampes. On August 2, in a general reunion of the clergy and bourgeois of Poitiers, it was decided to assemble the three orders of the province. The meeting of the estates of Poitou was held on August 20, and two delegates were chosen to carry the list of complaints and sug-

---

117   B. N., ms. fr. 20,084, p. 43.
118   A. C. Poitiers, K 7.

gestions to Etampes. These delegates met with the royal commissioners in Etampes from August 26 to September 6.[119] The results of their discussions are not known.

After the reign of Henry II, the three estates of Poitou did not meet again to discuss sending complaints to the king, except when called upon to prepare *cahiers* of grievances to be presented at meetings of the Estates General. It should be noted, however, that in addition to the opportunities afforded at assemblies of the Estates General, the clergy of Poitou had another means of presenting grievances to the king. After 1561, regular assemblies were held of the clergy of France. As a rule, the clergy of each diocese met, chose delegates and prepared lists of grievances for the general assembly.

Numerous assemblies of the clergy of the three dioceses approximately coterminous with Poitou were held for this purpose. For example, the clergy of the diocese of Maillezais met on May 4, 1573, to grant a mandate to the archbishop of Bordeaux and the bishop of Maillezais to represent them at an assembly of prelates already in progress in Paris.[120] The king had chosen these two men to represent the entire ecclesiastical province of Bordeaux and had instructed each diocese of the province to grant them a mandate. The clergy of Maillezais also prepared a list of grievances to be presented at this assembly of prelates. Some time during 1573 or 1574, the clergy of the diocese of Poitiers assembled to prepare a list of grievances to be presented to the king and to revoke a procuration previously given to certain prelates.[121] Numerous other examples could be cited of assemblies of the clergy of the diocese of Poitiers meeting for this purpose from 1561 down through the reign of Louis XIV.[122] Long after the three estates of Poitou had met for the last time, the clergy of the province retained this means of presenting their grievances to the king.[123]

[119] Ledain, "Maires de Poitiers", 432.

[120] *A. H. P.*, XX, 352-61. The assembly at Paris, originally scheduled for May 20, was advanced to April 30.

[121] *Ibid.*, 361-68. The beginning and end of the document are missing, but it can be dated approximately from internal evidence. The reference to the procuration given to certain prelates might refer to the mandate given to the archbishop of Bordeaux and the bishop of Maillezais for the assembly of prelates of April 30, 1573.

[122] A. D. Vienne, G 398, G 402, and G 403.

[123] It should be noted that diocesan synods continued to meet at least once a year to handle local church business, just as they had since the thirteenth century. See Doucet, II, 724. For such synods in the diocese of Poitiers, see A. D. Vienne, G 398-403.

D. RATIFICATION OF TREATIES

An interesting activity of the estates of Poitou was the ratification of treaties made by the King of France with foreign powers. It met three times for this purpose in c. December 1482, on March 28, 1497, and on November 27, 1529.

On the first occasion, it ratified the Treaty of Arras signed by Louis XI on December 23, 1482 with Maximilian of Hapsburg, which brought to an end the long struggle between the French king and Burgundy. Article 89 stipulated that the treaty was to be ratified by the three estates of France and by the estates of the provinces of the Low Countries. It was not stipulated that the three estates of all France must be assembled together and Louis XI chose to have the treaty ratified by the local estates separately.

The three estates of Poitou met in Poitiers and gave their assent to the treaty. The date of the assembly is not indicated but it probably took place some time during the month of December 1482, possibly even before the actual date of the signing of the treaty (December 23.) [124] The latest possible date on which the assembly in Poitiers could have taken place would be January 22, 1483, the date of the formal ratification by Louis XI.

The next treaty to be ratified by the three estates of Poitou was the Treaty of Etaples of November 3, 1492, which ended a brief war between France and England. The treaty called for perpetual peace between the two countries and the continuance of an annual pension previously promised by Louis XI to the English king. It was stipulated that it should be ratified within twelve months by the English parliament and the three estates of France.[125] On December 3, 1492, it was agreed that the ratification would be postponed until the next assembly of the three estates, provided that this meeting took place within three years.[126] If the estates had not met by this time, the king of France

---

[124] Royal letters convoking the estates of other provinces for this purpose are all dated early in December, e.g. letter summoning estates of Beaucaire, December 3 (assembly took place December 17); letter summoning estates of Ponthieu, December 3; letter summoning estates of Senlis, December 4. *Lettres de Louis XI, roi de France*, ed. J. Vaësen and E. Charavay, *Société de l'Histoire de France*, X (1908), 27-31.

[125] Ratificata et jurata per tres status regni sui Franciae, videlicet per praelatos et clerum, nobiles et civitates ejusdem regni rite et debite convocatus, *Ordonnances des rois de France de la troisième race* (Paris, 1860), XX, 364.

[126] P. Pélicier, ed., *Lettres de Charles VIII, roi de France, Société de l'Histoire de France* (Paris, 1905), V, 16, note 2.

reserved the right to have the treaty ratified by each of the provincial estates of the kingdom. As Charles VIII did not summon the Estates General within the three years stipulated, he decided to follow the alternative procedure, and sent copies of the treaty to each of the local estates of France with instructions to "confirm, ratify and approve, and to observe, maintain and keep" the said treaty.[127]

Accordingly, André de Vivonne (incorrectly called by Rymer, Andre Devuionne), seigneur de la Chasteignerai, seneschal of Poitou, assembled in Poitiers on March 28, 1497, the clergy, nobles, bourgeois, and inhabitants of the good towns and places of the *sénéchaussée* to ratify the articles of the treaty. He stated that he was acting in accordance with royal letters patent which he had received. The articles of the treaty and the royal instructions were read. The latter left little chance for discussion or opposition. The deputies were tersely instructed to ratify the treaty. The seneschal and the estates of Poitou confirmed and approved all of the articles. On June 17, 1499, the King of France received the ratification of the Treaty of Etaples from the English ambassador.[128] He then presented to the latter the documents of ratification by eighteen local and provincial estates of France, including those of Poitou, and by thirty-eight great personages of the kingdom. In order to complete the ratification, the King of France still had to deliver the documents of ratification from a number of other local estates, which are listed.

The third occasion on which the estates of Poitou was summoned to ratify a treaty was in November 1529. The rather complicated circumstances require some explanation. The king, Francis I, had been captured at the Battle of Pavia in 1525 by the armies of the Emperor Charles V. In order to secure his release, he was forced to agree to the treaty of Madrid of January 4, 1526, by which he ceded Burgundy and other territories to Charles and agreed to send his two young sons to Spain as hostages to ensure that the terms were carried out. As soon as he was released, Francis claimed that the treaty was invalid because he had agreed to it under compulsion, and renewed the war. Finally, a new peace was concluded, the Treaty of Cambrai of August 3, 1529. It renewed many of the clauses of the Treaty of Madrid, the chief exception being that France retained Burgundy. It also stipulated that Francis' two sons would be freed in return for a payment of two million *écus d'or*. It was agreed that the Treaty of Cambrai would be ratified by the

---

[127] Thomas Rymer, *Foedera, conventiones, litterae, et cujuscunque generis acta publica* (Hague Comitis, 1741), V, part 2, 89, hereafter cited as Rymer.
[128] A. N., P. 2302, pp. 789-92.

various particular estates of France. They would also ratify those articles of the Treaty of Madrid which were not altered by the new agreement.

Accordingly, the three estates of Poitou met in Lusignan on November 27, 1529, and ratified the two treaties. The assembly was presided over by François de la Trémoïlle, royal lieutenant in Poitou and Saintonge, and François Doyneau, lieutenant general of Poitou. The act of ratification by the estates of Poitou has not survived. Copies of the acts of ratification by the estates of the *baillages* of Montferrand, Berry, Montargis, Orleans and numerous other regions, have been preserved, however.[129] In each case the wording is almost identical. Hence, in all probability, the act of ratification by the estates of Poitou was very similar. In all cases the king stipulated the precise form of the oath which the estates were to swear, leaving little possibility for discussion. They were to promise to observe the Treaty of Cambrai and the Treaty of Madrid to the extent that the latter was not altered by the former. On March 1, 1530, Marguerite, Archduchess of Austria, acknowledged on behalf of Charles V, receipt from the French ambassador of the ratifications by the various estates of France of the two treaties.[130] The latter were listed and included sealed letters, dated November 27, 1529, containing ratification of these treaties by the three estates of the "*pays, province* and *sénéchaussée*" of Poitou.

Ledain, drawing his information from the sixteenth century Poitevin historian, Bouchet, states that, at the meeting at Lusignan of November 1529, the estates of Poitou also voted the sum necessary for their share of the king's ransom and the delivery of his children.[131] All other information seems to indicate, however, that this was not true. A memoir from Francis I, dated April 1526, to the governors of the different regions of France stated that the royal council had decided that everyone should help pay the ransom, including the clergy.[132] The tax was to be apportioned in the same manner as the *tailles*; that is to say, by the estates in the *pays d'états*, and by the *élus* elsewhere. The share of the nobles and the clergy was to be settled by negotiation.

Francis I obtained express permission from the Pope to tax the clergy and they were assessed at the rate of four *livres* per ten on their bene-

---

[129]   B. N., ms. fr. 3086, fols. 98-121; *Ibid.*, n.a. 1118, fols. 135-142; *Ibid.*, ms. fr. 6199, no. 3.
[130]   *Ordonnances des rois de France, règne de François I er, Académie des Sciences Morales et Politiques*, VI, part I, 72-73.
[131]   Ledain, "Maires de Poitiers", p. 519; Bouchet, p. 453.
[132]   B. N., ms. fr. 15,637, fols. 120-28.

fices.[133] In Poitou the details were left in the hands of the bishop of Poitiers.[134]

A large assembly of nobles at Paris offered the king one tenth of the revenues from their *fiefs* and *arrière-fiefs* for one year. The king then sent out letters convoking assemblies of the nobles in all of the different *baillages* and *sénéchaussées* of France requesting them to make a similar offer.[135] The nobles of Poitou made the grant as requested, stipulating that it was not to be considered as a precedent.[136] Some time in late 1529 or early 1530, the nobles of Poitou must have held an assembly to grant this tax. Considerable information is available about its apportionment amongst the various nobles of the province.[137] During February and March 1530, they went on appointed days to various centers to swear to the value of their revenues.

All of the *roturiers* (those who normally paid the *tailles*) of France were taxed to pay the ransom and even the free towns (*villes franches*) were asked to contribute.[138] Poitiers, which at the time belonged to the latter group, was asked to pay 10,000 *livres*.[139] However, the mayor of Poitiers, René Berthelot, made a special trip to Blois and persuaded the king and the royal council to reduce the town's contribution to 6000 *livres*.[140]

In all probability then, the three estates of Poitou did not vote the province's share of the royal ransom. The clergy was assessed directly by the king with papal approval. The nobles of Poitou probably did assemble and agree to grant the tax requested by the king. The *roturiers* were assessed by the *élus* and the free towns, such as Poitiers, were asked to contribute, although their share was apparently subject to negotiation.

---

[133] *Ibid.*, fols. 189-92. Also *Ibid.*, ms. fr. 5,497, fol. 265, r°. In other words, they would pay four *décimes*.

[134] Bouchet, p. 453.

[135] B. N., ms. fr. 15,637, fols. 154-56 and 189-92. See also ms. fr. 5,497, fol. 265 v°.

[136] Bouchet, p. 453.

[137] A. D. Deux-Sèvres, C 12, published in part by H. Ravan, "Etat des nobles du Poitou à l'occasion de l'aide extraordinaire offerte par eux à F. de la Trémoïlle, Commissaire général du Roi en Poitou et Saintonge, pour le rachat de la rançon du Roi François I er après la bataille de Pavie, *Mémoires de la Société de statistique du département des Deux-Sèvres*, ser. 2, I (1860-61), 59-81. Also B. N., ms. fr. 15,637, fols. 209-213.

[138] *Ibid.*, fols. 189-92.

[139] *Ibid.*, fols. 205-08.

[140] A. C. Poitiers, M., reg. 11, fol. 62 v°.

E. CODIFICATION OF CUSTOMS

Another function of the estates of Poitou was the codification of the provincial custom. In some provinces of southern France, written laws had been followed for many years. In the rest of France, however, unwritten custom was followed which varied considerably from place to place. Charles VII had inaugurated a royal policy of codifying the customs of these various provinces. The work was carried on slowly by his successors, especially Louis XII.

The three estates of Poitou met for this purpose on October 16, 1514, before two royal commissioners. An earlier codification of the customs of Poitou, compiled around 1417, seems to have served as a basis. This earlier codification had been made by a handful of Poitevin lawyers in Thouars, without royal authorization and without the participation of the estates of Poitou.[141] After the articles of the new compilation had been read one by one and approved by the assembly, the commissioners declared them to be law.

During the latter half of the sixteenth century, especially during the reign of Henry II, the customs of many provinces were recodified. As in the case of the previous codification, the three estates of the region in question were summoned. The estates of Poitou met for this purpose in Poitiers from October 16 to October 21, 1559.[142] The assembly was presided over by three royal commissioners, headed by Christofle de Thou, president in the Parlement of Paris, whose personal role in the recodification of the customs of many provinces was probably greater than that of any other individual.[143] The custom of Poitou, as codified in 1514, was used as a basis and changes consisted mainly of adding or removing a few words for greater clarity. The old custom was read, article by article, and the various changes made. In each case it was stated to what article in the old codification the new article corresponded. The deputies of the estates of Poitou do seem to have played a role in the recodification, as some alterations were made on their advice.

The procedure followed in the case of individual opposition to a particular article is interesting. The article was passed but those protesting were given a written acknowledgment of their protest. It was stated

---

[141] See René Filhol, *Le vieux Coustumier de Poictou* (Bourges, 1956).

[142] The *procès-verbal* of this assembly has been published by C. A. Bourdot de Richebourg, *Nouveau Coutumier général* (Paris, 1724), IV, 775-839, hereafter cited as Bourdot de Richebourg.

[143] See René Filhol, *Le premier président Christofle de Thou et la réformation des coutumes* (Paris, 1937).

that the article in question was to be enforced "without prejudice to their particular rights and titles, if they have any". Presumably they could then bring their alleged particular rights before the regular legal courts if they so desired.

Before the assembly adjourned on October 21, the commissioners declared this codification of custom to be the law of Poitou and stated that in future, no other custom could be pleaded in court. The commissioners presented a signed copy of this codification to the Parlement of Paris on April 22, 1560, and it was preserved in the registers of the Court of Parlement.

F. ELECTION OF DEPUTIES TO THE ESTATES GENERAL

The first time that the three estates of Poitou met to elect deputies to the Estates General was in about December 1483. Henceforth, the election of deputies and the preparation of lists of grievances for assemblies of the Estates General was one of their principal functions. In fact, after 1559, it was the only reason for which they were summoned. Between 1560 and 1651 they met seven times for this purpose.[144]

It has been said that election to the Estates General in France was generally considered more of a burden than a privilege. This was not always the case in Poitou. On one occasion at least, in 1651, election among the nobles was keenly sought. This is shown clearly by a letter, dated June 25, from the baron of Hervault, *châtelain* of Pleumartin, to the town council of Poitiers.[145] The baron was seeking their support for his candidature for deputy for the nobles. He mentioned the fact that many men "of merit and of high rank" were contesting this election. The hot disputes that occurred when the assembly of nobles was finally held on July 3, and the lengths to which one candidate, the marquis of la Rocheposay, went to obtain his election will be described in detail below.[146]

Let us examine now the type of men elected as deputies to the Estates General by the three estates of Poitou.[147] The clergy normally elected

---

[144] See Appendix A, Catalogue of Assemblies.
[145] Régistres de Poitiers, reg. 102, June 26, 1651. This is probably the same man as the marquis of Oirvau for whom many of the votes by proxy were cast in the assembly of the nobles held July 3 and July 4, 1651. See below, pp. 129-30.
[146] See below, pp. 127-
[147] No information is available about any of the deputies chosen in Poitou in 1561, or about those chosen by the nobles in 1560. Otherwise, the names of all the deputies can be determined.

either two or three deputies.[148] The only exception was in 1649 when only one man was chosen. On this latter occasion, they complied rather reluctantly with royal instructions, some clergymen complaining that they normally chose two deputies, one from the higher clergy (bishops and abbots) and one from the lower. This, indeed, seems to have been their usual procedure. On every other occasion, except in 1483 and 1576, they elected one member of the higher clergy (either a bishop or an abbot) and one of the lower clergy.[149] When they followed this practice, the deputy from the higher clergy always came from outside the town of Poitiers with either the bishop of Luçon or the bishop of Maillezais being the most frequent choice. Every deputy from the lower clergy throughout the entire period came from the town of Poitiers. They were always deans or canons from either the cathedral of Poitiers or the Chapter of St. Hilaire-le-Grand. Hence, the clergy of the town of Poitiers was always represented by one, sometimes two, and on one occasion three deputies.[150] The only delegate elected by the clergy of Poitou who later achieved national fame was Armand-Jean du Plessis de Richelieu, whom they chose in 1614.

The nobles of Poitou always elected either one or two deputies.[151]

---

[148] The following are the sources of information about the deputies elected by the clergy in Poitou: 1483 – Jean Masselin, *Journal des Etats Généraux tenus à Tours en 1484 sous le règne de Charles VIII*, ed. A. Bernier, *Collection de documents inédits sur l'histoire de France* (Paris, 1835), Appendix V, pp. 724-25, hereafter cited as Masselin; Charles Mayer, *Des Etats Généraux et autres assemblées nationales* (The Hague, 1788-89), VII, 398, hereafter cited as Mayer; 1560 – *A. H. P.*, XX, 325-34; 1576 – A. D. Vienne, G 399, Oct. 1, 1576; B. N. ms. fr. n. a. 7853; Mayer, XIII, 151-52; 1588. – *Ibid.*, XIV, 320-21; 1614 – Toussaint Quinet, *Recueil général des estats tenus en France sous les Rois Charles VI, Charles VIII, Henry III, et Louis XIII* (Paris, 1651), pp. 252-53, hereafter cited as Quinet; G. Hanotaux, "La Jeunesse de Richelieu", *Revue des Deux Mondes*, XCIV (Aug. 1, 1889), 600; G. Hanotaux, *Histoire du Cardinal de Richelieu* (Paris, 1896), I, 150; Abbé L. Lacroix, "Richelieu à Luçon – Sa jeunesse, son épiscopat", *M. S. A. O.*, Ser. 2, XII (1889), 283, hereafter cited as Lacroix, "Richelieu à Luçon", *M. S. A. O.*, XII; 1649 – A. D. Vienne, G 411, Feb. 26, 1649; 1651 – *Ibid.*, July 3, 1651.

[149] In 1483 both deputies were bishops. In 1576, all three deputies were deans or canons.

[150] In 1576 all three deputies came from Poitiers.

[151] The following are the sources of information about the deputies elected by the nobles of Poitou; 1483 – Masselin, Appendix V, pp. 724-25; A. N., KK 648, fol. 92, no. 85; 1576 – Mayer, XIII, 151-52; 1588 – *Ibid.*, XIV, 320-21; Régistres de Poitiers, reg. 48, Feb. 10, 1589; H. Ouvré, "Essai sur l'histoire de la Ligue à Poitiers", *M. S. A. O.*, ser. 1, XXI (1854), 148-49, hereafter cited as Ouvré, "Essai sur la Ligue à Poitiers", *M. S. A. O.*, XXI; 1614 – Quinet, 252-53; 1649 – Régistres de Poitiers, reg. 100, March 1, 1649; *Journal de M. Demaillasson, avocat du roi à Montmorillon*, ed. V. Bardet, *A. H. P.*, XXXVI, 6, hereafter cited as *Journal*

Among them can be found members of the greatest noble families of Poitou, such as Georges de la Trémoïlle, seigneur de Royan, René, count of Sanzay, hereditary viscount and *parageur* of Poitou, Charles de Vivonne, seigneur de la Chateigneraye, and Benjamin de la Rochechouart, baron of Estissac. On one occasion, in 1651, they elected the royal lieutenant in Poitou, the marquis of la Rocheposay.

The number of deputies elected by the third estate varied from one to four.[152] The majority of them were royal legal or administrative officials, although in 1614 one merchant was included. At least one deputy always came from the town of Poitiers and sometimes their representation was even higher.[153] Out of a total of six deputies elected in 1614, 1649, and 1651, five were from Poitiers. A number of the men elected, such as Maurice Claveurier in 1483, and Pierre Rat in 1576, belonged to the most distinguished bourgeois families in Poitiers.

Due to the relative infrequency of the meetings of the Estates General, it is not surprising that very few men were elected as deputy on more than one occasion.[154] As nearly as can be determined, only four men achieved this distinction in Poitou. As might be expected, two of these cases of reelection occured in 1651. Only two years had elapsed since the previous election of deputies and the royal instructions offered the option of either renewing the mandate of those chosen in 1649, or choosing new delegates. Mathieu Thoreau, dean of the Cathedral of Poitiers, was reelected by the clergy, and Maître Florentin Roatin, sieur de Jorigny, judge magistrate and dean of the royal councillors in Poitiers, was reelected by the third estate. Anthoine de la Sayette, canon

---

de M. Demaillasson, *A. H. P.*, XXXVI; 1651 – Mss. de la Bibliothèque de Poitiers, 304 (42); Régistres de Poitiers, reg. 102, July 3, 1651.

[152] The following are the sources of information about deputies elected by the third estate: 1483 – Masselin, Appendix V, pp. 724-25; Bélisaire Ledain, *Histoire sommaire de la ville de Poitiers* (Fontenay-le-Comte, 1889), p. 134; B. N., p.o. vol. 772, doss. 17,625, Claveurier, no. 15; 1576 – Mayer, XIII, 151-52; 1588 – *Ibid.*, XIV, 320-21; 1614 – Quinet, pp. 252-53; 1649 – *Journal de M. Demaillasson, A. H. P.*, XXXVI, 6; Régistres de Poitiers, reg. 100, March 1, 1649; 1651 – *Ibid.*, reg. 102, July 3, 1651; Mss. de la Bibliothèque de Poitiers, 304 (42).

[153] As will be seen later, certain areas of Poitou sometimes attempted to send their own deputies directly to meetings of the Estates General. This explains in part the apparently disproportionately high representation of the town of Poitiers among the deputies elected at the meeting of the three estates of the province. For example, in 1649 the only deputy elected for the third estate at the meeting of the estates of Poitou came from Poitiers, but this does not give the complete picture because the secondary jurisdiction of Fontenay-le-Comte was sending its own delegation.

[154] It should be remembered that no information is available on the deputies elected in 1561. It is possible that some of those chosen in 1560 were reelected.

and later dean of the Cathedral of Poitiers, was elected by the clergy in both 1560 and 1576. The most interesting case, however, is that of Georges de la Trémoïlle, seigneur de Royan, abbot of Chambon and Saint-Laon de Thouars, who was elected by the clergy in 1560 and by the nobles in 1576.

It is interesting to note the political leanings of the deputies elected by the three estates of Poitou during the troubled period of the Fronde. Of the three delegates chosen in 1649, the only one who might be regarded as a supporter of Mazarin was Mathieu Thoreau, the deputy from the clergy. The deputy from the second estate, the baron of Estissac, was a turbulent noble not noted for his loyalty to Mazarin or the king. The election of Florentin Roatin by the third estate was the principal triumph for the partisans of the Fronde. He was not a violent *Frondeur,* but did belong to a group of the bourgeoisie that had lent considerable money to the monarchy and was anxious to see royal expenses controlled by the Parlement.[155] In 1651 both deputies from the clergy and both deputies from the nobles might be considered supporters of the king and the queen mother. The two deputies from the third estate were inclined to support the pretensions of the Parlement of Paris.[156]

The only information available about the type of mandate given the deputies elected in Poitou concerns the delegates from the first estate. The clergy invested their deputies with very wide powers, limited only by the contents of their *cahier.* On October 11, 1576, they gave their three deputies letters patent granting them full powers and special mandate to act for the clergy of Poitou and do "all that they would do and could do if they were all present (tous ce quilz feroient et faire pourroient si tous ensemble y estoient)".[157] Moreover, the clergy of Poitou committed themselves in advance to agree to any promises which their deputies might make at the Estates General. The assembly of October 1, 1576 concluded by stating that it was granting its deputies "full powers and special mandate" (plains pouvoirs et mandement special)" to act according to their consciences in the interests of the clergy of Poitou. In 1560 also, the clergy granted its delegates the same wide powers and committed itself in advance to abide by anything they might agree

---

[155] G. Debien, "La question des Etats Généraux de 1649 et de 1651. La convocation et les élections en Haut-Poitou", *B. S. A. O.*, ser. 3, X (1934-35), 612-13, hereafter cited as Debien, "La question des Etats Généraux de 1649 et de 1651", *B. S. A. O.*, X.

[156] *Ibid.*, 629.

[157] A. D. Vienne, G 399, Oct. 1, 1576.

to at the Estates General.[158] Clearly then, this might be described as a mandate of *plena potestas*.

As for the payment of deputies, once again, most of the information available concerns the first estate. In 1483, 1560 and 1576, the clergy of Poitou promised to pay all of the expenses of their deputies.[159] It is probable that this was their normal practice.

The procedure followed by the other two orders varied.[160] In 1484 the deputies from both the nobles and the third estate in Poitou seem to have paid out of the regular *taille*.[161] The deputies from all three orders who had attended the Estates General of 1560 were to be paid from a special tax imposed by the king.[162] Royal letters of January 30, 1561 stipulated that this tax was to be divided among the clergy in accordance with the *décimes*, among the nobles in accordance with the *arrière-ban*, and among the third estate in accordance with the *taille*, except that the free towns would also contribute.[163] The tax was to be apportioned in each *baillage* or *sénéchaussé*e by a committee of six persons from each estate chosen at the assembly of the three estates of that region called to elect deputies to the Estates General of 1561.

An interesting case occurred following the Estates General of 1588 which shows that the procedure for the payment of the deputies of the second estate in Poitou was by no means constant. In a disputed election, the count of Sanzay had been elected as deputy for the second estate by the *échevins* of Poitiers and some other nobles.[164] Both he and a rival candidate attended the Estates General and were accepted by the king. On February 10, 1589, the count appeared before the town council of Poitiers. He stated that his trip to attend the Estates General had cost him a lot of money and he requested that the town of Poitiers

---

[158] *A. H. P.*, XX, 325-34.

[159] Masselin, p. 498; Mayer, VII, 398; *A. H. P.*, XX, 325-34; A. D. Vienne, G 399, Oct. 1, and Oct. 17, 1576.

[160] For a good general treatment of this topic, see J. R. Major, "The Payment Of The Deputies To The French National Assemblies, 1484-1627", *Journal of Modern History*, XXVII (1955), 217-20, hereafter cited as Major "The Payment of Deputies", *J. M. H.*, XXVII.

[161] Guillaume d'Appelvoisin, sire de Pigny, and Maurice Claveurier, deputies from the second and third estates respectively, each acknowledged receipt of three hundred *livres tournois* from the receiver of the *tailles* in Poitou for having attented the Estates General of 1484. A. N., KK 648, fol. 92, no. 85; B. N., p.o., vol. 772, doss. 17,625: Claveurier, no. 15.

[162] Major, "The Payment of Deputies", *J. M. H.*, XXVII, 217-20.

[163] *Ibid.*

[164] See below, pp. 126-27.

reimburse him.[165] Whether the town did so or not cannot be determined.

The attempts made by various parts of Poitou to send separate delegations to the Estates General constitute a final matter which must be examined before leaving the topic of the election of deputies. As a rule these efforts were unsuccessful. The most frequent attempts were made by the inhabitants of the secondary *sénéchaussée* of Fontenay-le-Comte. In 1588 they sent two deputies from the third estate directly to Blois where they were permitted to present their *cahier*.[166] In 1614 they also sent two deputies directly to the Estates General. In the ensuing argument, their pretensions were supported by the bishop of Maillezais. The royal decision, however, forced them to turn over their *cahiers* to the properly elected deputies of the third estate of Poitou.[167] In 1649 Fontenay-le-Comte again claimed the right to a special delegation and refused to participate in the assembly of the three estates of Poitou.[168] Possibly one reason for their continuous refusal to join with the rest of the province in the election of deputies was bitterness over the fact that opposition from the town of Poitiers had prevented them in 1598 and again in 1644, from getting a separate presidial seat of justice detached from that of Poitiers.

Several other regions or groups in Poitou occasionally tried to send separate delegations to the Estates General. In 1576 the secondary *baillage* of Montmorillon sent deputies of its own to Blois. The delegates elected by the three estates of Poitou protested. The king decided that, since in the past the estates of Poitou had been convoked at Poitiers for the entire province, the delegates from Montmorillon would not be admitted. They were instructed to turn over their *cahiers* to the properly elected delegates from Poitou.[169] In 1614 the bishop of Poitiers informed Richelieu that the clergy of the diocese of Maillezais was planning to hold a separate election at Fontenay-le-Comte and send its own deputies to Paris. He assured Richelieu that they would not succeed, however.[170] The clergy of Luçon sent their own deputy to the Estates General in 1576. An interesting case occurred in 1588 when the chapter

[165]   Régistres de Poitiers, reg. 48, Feb. 10, 1589.
[166]   Mayer, XIV, 320-21.
[167]   Archives historiques de Fontenay-le-Comte, III, 271-72.
[168]   Debien, "La question des Etats Généraux de 1649 et de 1651", *B.S.A.O.*, X, 609.
[169]   B. N., ms. fr. 23,935, p. 226.
[170]   Hanotaux, "La Jeunesse de Richelieu", *Revue des Deux Mondes*, XCIV, 600; Hanotaux, *Histoire du Cardinal de Richelieu*, I, 150.

of Saint-Hilaire-le-Grand in Poitiers claimed that the clergy of Poitou had not accepted its *cahier*. Therefore, they chose one of their canons to go in person to the meeting of the Estates General and present it.[171] Whether he actually went cannot be determined.[172]

G. REGIONAL ASSEMBLIES
WITH THE ESTATES OF OTHER PROVINCES

Yet another activity of the estates of Poitou was its participation in joint assemblies with the estates of other provinces. It is questionable whether or not such assemblies should be discussed in a history of the estates of Poitou, or whether they should more properly be thought of as fractional meetings of the Estates General. Regional assemblies of this type seem to be intermediate in nature between Estates General and provincial estates and merit a special study.

Prior to 1560, the estates of Poitou participated in at least thirteen joint meetings with the estates of neighbouring provinces,[173] exclusive of assemblies of the Estates of Languedoil. Nine of these assemblies took place between 1416 and 1464 and their purpose varied considerably. The other four were held between the years 1549 and 1553 concerning salt taxes. In addition, it is probable that several other joint meetings regarding salt taxes were held in this latter four-year period. After 1560, there is no record of any further regional assemblies involving Poitou, unless one includes the meeting at Angoulême of March 20, 1561 of the northern half of the government of Guyenne, held to elect deputies to the Estates General.

The estates of Saintonge participated, along with the estates of Poitou, in all thirteen of these regional assemblies about which information is available. On three occasions, only the estates of these two provinces were involved. On the other ten occasions the estates of one or more other provinces also met with them. The estates of Angoumois participated eight times, those of Haute Marche five times, those of Basse Marche four times,[174] those of Périgord four times, those of the town

---

[171] Collection Dom Fonteneau, LX, 457.

[172] Mayer does not include him in his list of deputies. Mayer, XIV, 320-21.

[173] May 1416, May 1418, November 25, 1421, December 20, 1425, May 1, 1426, 1433, August 1434, c. 1451-1454, January 10, 1464, July 11, 1549, November 1549 (two meetings), and October 1, 1553.

[174] The estates of La Marche referred to in documents dating from the reign of Charles VII were, in reality, only the estates of Haute Marche, as Basse Marche,

and *gouvernement* of La Rochelle four times, those of Anjou three times, those of Touraine three times, those of Châtellerault three times, and those of Maine twice. The participation of the estates of Limousin is more difficult to analyze because the documents describing the joint assemblies in the fifteenth century refer only to the estates of Limousin, while those describing the sixteenth century assemblies are more specific and distinguish between the estates of Haut Limousin and Bas Limousin. During the fifteenth century, the estates of Limousin were involved in three of the joint assemblies. The estates of Haut Limousin took part in all four assemblies between 1549 and 1553, while the estates of Bas Limousin only took part in three. In addition, the estates of several tiny regions such as Combrailles and Franc-Alleu participated in at least one of these meetings regarding the salt taxes. It is possible that the estates of Guyenne were also involved in these latter assemblies. Of the thirteen definite regional assemblies, eight were held in Poitou and four in one of the other provinces involved. The location of the joint meeting which took place c. 1451-54 cannot be ascertained.

Unfortunately, very little is known about the way in which Poitou was represented at these regional assemblies. The town of Poitiers sent delegates to the joint meeting of the estates of Poitou and Saintonge in December 1425.[175] The assembly of May 1, 1426, to which the estates of Poitou, Saintonge, Anjou, Maine, Limousin, and Touraine had been summoned, was very poorly attended. Several barons and members of the clergy from Poitou were present but the only town represented was Angers.[176] At the meeting of January 10, 1464, one man, Denis Dausseure, an *échevin* from Poitiers, represented all three estates of Poitou.[177] How he was chosen cannot be determined. The royal letters patent calling for the regional assembly of July 11, 1549, instructed each town to elect three deputies, one from each estate.[178] Poitiers complied with these instructions. On November 11, 1549, the estates of Périgord met and chose three members of the clergy, two nobles, and three members of the third estate to represent them at the regional assembly to be held in Poitiers later that month.[179] One may perhaps conjecture that the

---

at the time, was divided, for financial purposes, between Poitou and Bas Limousin. Thomas, *Les Etats provinciaux*, p. 179.

[175] Régistres de Poitiers, reg. 2, fol. 72, Jan. 4, 1426.

[176] Beaucourt, II, 588-89.

[177] B. N., ms. fr. 20,084, p. 46. Also Régistres de Poitiers, reg. 4, fol. 123. Jan. 17, 1464.

[178] *Ibid.*, reg. 30, July 6, 1549.

[179] B. N., Collection de Périgord, XXIV, fol. 336.

representation of Poitou at this meeting would be similar. All that is known about the deputies from Poitou at the regional assembly of October 1, 1553, is that they were chosen by the three estates of the province at a meeting held on September 25.[180] Probably they were relatively few in number.

It is evident that the representation of Poitou at regional assemblies was by no means consistent in nature throughout the entire period under study. It appears that in 1425 and 1426 those who attended were the type of delegates who would normally attend an assembly of the three estates of Poitou meeting alone. In January 1464, July 1549, November 1549 and October 1553, the province seems to have been represented by a small number of delegates, however, chosen on at least one occasion by the estates of Poitou. Although evidence is too limited to permit certainty, one is tempted to speculate that the regional assemblies during the reign of Charles VII were, in effect, combined meetings of the three estates of various provinces to which all were summoned who would normally be invited to attend an assembly of the three estates of any of the provinces meeting separately. From the reign of Louis XI on, however, they seem to have changed in nature, and the representation appears to have become more of the type to be found at a meeting of the Estates General with each province represented by a few deputies from each order.

A thorough examination of the local archives of the other provinces involved in these regional assemblies would undoubtedly throw further light on this interesting subject.

H.   OTHER ACTIVITIES

The three estates of Poitou occasionally engaged in other activities which cannot be classified among any of the categories already described. For example, in June 1417, they were instructed to swear obedience to the dauphin Charles as their "natural lord who had recently succeeded to his land and seigneury of Poitou".[181] No other examples can be cited, however, of the three estates of Poitou being called upon to swear allegience to a new lord. On one occasion, between the years 1451 and 1453, the estates of Poitou met jointly with those of Saintonge and

---

[180]   Collection Dom Fonteneau, XXVII, ter. 141.
[181]   A. C. Poitiers, J 554.

Angoumois to make arrangements for workers to bring back into cultivation lands in these provinces which had been ruined by the years of
warfare.[182] This is the only known instance of the three estates of Poitou
engaging in this kind of activity.

[182]   A. N., X2a 41, plaidoiries du 4 mars, 1477. The document states that this took
place after the French conquest of Guyenne, but does not indicate whether this
means the first conquest in 1451 or the reconquest in 1453.

III

ORGANIZATION AND PROCEDURE

A. THE SUMMONS

As a rule, the three estates of Poitou were summoned by their feudal lord. From 1372 until his death in 1416, Poitou formed part of the apanage of John, duke of Berry, and it was normally he who issued the orders calling for an assembly of the estates.[1] From 1416 to 1422, the dauphin Charles, as count of Poitou, usually convoked the meetings.[2] When he became king in 1422, Poitou escheated to the royal domain and henceforth it was normally the king who summoned the three estates of the province.

There were, however, some exceptions to the general rule, most of them occurring before 1470. In November 1390 and November 1391, the three estates of Poitou were summoned by the count of Montpensier, son of John, duke of Berry. It is to be assumed, however, that he was merely acting under authority delegated by his father. On four occasions, in 1404, 1409, December 1425, and May 1426, the three estates of the province were summoned by the constable of France, commander of the royal armies.[3] Whether he was acting on his own initiative or merely as a royal commissioner, cannot be determined. In 1549 Anthony of Bourbon, King of Navarre, acting as lieutenant governor of Guyenne, wrote to the seneschal of Poitou and various other royal and municipal officials of the *sénéchaussée*. He invited them to send two of their number or any others who might be elected by the people of the province, to an assembly at Tarbes on April 28, 1549 of deputies from all of the

---

[1] In 1393, 1395, 1396, 1399, July 1411, September 1412, November 1412, December 1412, May 1413, and May 1415. For all sources not specifically cited for references to particular assemblies of the estates of Poitou in this chapter, see Appendix A, Catalogue of Assemblies, under the appropriate date.

[2] As in November 1416, June 1417, May 1418, and October 1418.

[3] By Charles d'Albret in 1404 and 1409. By Arthur de Richemont in December 1425 and May 1426.

provinces under his jurisdiction.[4] This one letter is the only information available. The nature of the assembly, if it ever took place, cannot be determined. If it was an assembly of estates, then this might be considered an example of someone other than the king convoking the estates of Poitou. The King of Navarre may, however, have been acting under royal instructions.

By far the most interesting exception to the rule was the convocation of the three estates of Poitou on a number of occasions by the town council of Poitiers. This happened at least six times between the years 1446 and 1461.[5] This procedure would be unusual at any time but what makes it especially surprising is the fact that it occurred during the latter years of the reign of Charles VII. Historians, when describing this period, generally depict a royal government, jealous of its prerogatives, steadily strangling representative institutions and bringing the control of local affairs more and more into the hands of the central government. It is true that the fate of the Estates General does, to some extent, justify this interpretation. Also many of the provincial estates, including those of Poitou, had lost the right to vote royal taxes. However, the fact that the town council of Poitiers was able to summon the estates of the province on six occasions during a fifteen year period, may perhaps be interpreted to mean that the alleged royal policy of centralization and the accompanying decay of provincial estates, had not gone as far as is generally supposed. Certainly it shows the prestige and the dominant position of the town of Poitiers within the province.

Two other cases can be cited when the town of Poitiers summoned the three estates of Poitou. In 1466 Louis XI instructed the clergy and bourgeois of the town to send a written list of grievances on several specific matters to a group of royal commissioners at Etampes. The clergy and bourgeois of Poitiers met on August 2, and decided to assemble the three estates of the province to add their grievances.[6] The assembly took place on August 20. The other case occurred on September 25, 1553 when the estates of Poitou met once again at the summons of the town of Poitiers. This time, however, this procedure had been specifically authorized by the king. He had sent commissioners to Saintes with authorization to instruct various municipal officials of the chief

---

[4] *A. H. P.*, IV, 314-15.
[5] November 10, 1446; November 1447; late 1450; April 1454; July 18, 1454; August 9, 1461.
[6] Régistres de Poitiers, reg. 6, Aug. 2, 1466.

towns of Poitou and other neighbouring regions to assemble the estates of their respective provinces.[7]

Whenever the king, or feudal lord, decided to assemble the three estates of Poitou, his first step was to issue letters patent to the official or officials who would preside. These letters instructed the latter to assemble the estates and stated the purpose of the meeting. During the sixteenth and seventeenth centuries, they were usually fairly specific about the role to be played by the estates. During the reign of Charles VII, they were not always so clear, however. For example, when it was a question of levying a tax, Thomas found that the royal letters patent sometimes neglected to mention the estates at all and merely instructed the commissioners to impose it.[8] In some such cases, other documents proved, however, that the estates did meet to consent to the tax. In some areas, during the reign of Charles VII, the commissioners also received letters close signed by the king to accredit them to the estates. None of these letters close for Poitou has been discovered but one for Lyons has survived and is perhaps typical.[9]

Once they had received the royal instructions, the presiding officers summoned the three estates of Poitou. The means by which they did so changed somewhat during the long period under study. During the first half of the fifteenth century, they sent letters close to the clergy, nobles and towns of the province notifying them of the assembly and inviting them to attend or, in the case of the towns, abbeys or chapters, to send delegates. In November 1412, two sergeants of the duke of Berry bore these letters. One carried them to the barons and the other to the prelates, clergy and towns. In December 1412 the procedure was almost identical, one sergeant bearing letters close to the barons and several *chevaliers*, and the other to the prelates and towns.[10] The procedure was similar even when the king had not authorized the assembly or appointed any presiding officers, as in November 1447, when the three estates of Poitou were summoned by the town council of Poitiers.[11] On this occasion, the town council sent letters close to various seigneurs and towns inviting them to attend or send delegates. The means by which they summoned the clergy was not indicated but they were represented. None of the letters close convoking an assembly of the estates of Poitou during the first half of the fifteenth century has sur-

---

[7] A. C. Poitiers, C 33; Collection Dom Fonteneau, XXVII, ter., 141.
[8] Thomas, *Les Etats provinciaux*, pp. 59-61.
[9] *Ibid.*, pp. 61-62.
[10] Lacour, "Une incursion anglaise", *A. H. P.*, XLVIII, 82-83.
[11] Régistres de Poitiers, reg. 3, fol. 89.

vived. One such letter to a noble of Anjou, announcing a meeting of the three estates of that province in 1426, has been discovered, however, and is probably typical.[12]

The only information available on the way in which the summons was issued locally in Poitou between the years 1461 and 1559 concerns the assembly of September 25, 1553.[13] The mayor, peers, *échevins,* and bourgeois of Poitiers were invited to attend by the presiding officer. The town council then chose two sergeants to issue the summons for the *châtellenie* of Poitiers. Notices were then printed announcing the assembly to the town and *châtellenie* at a cost of 60 *sols tournois.* The means by which the summons was issued to the rest of the province cannot be determined.

Considerably more information is available on the method of summons for assemblies of the three estates of Poitou called to elect deputies to the Estates General between the years 1560 and 1651. The procedure followed in the various *baillages* and *sénéchaussées* of France was fairly complex.[14] Before the general assembly of the three estates of the *baillage* or *sénéchaussée* was held, a number of important preliminary steps were necessary.

In Poitou the royal letters of convocation were addressed to the seneschal or his lieutenant general. As a rule it was the latter who received and acted upon them. These letters stated the purpose, date and place of meeting of the Estates General and called for an assembly of the three estates of the *sénéchaussée* to elect deputies. Usually the number of deputies to be elected was specified. The seneschal or his lieutenant general then fixed the date for the assembly and issued letters of convocation.

For example, early in February 1649, Claude de Tudert, lieutenant general of Poitou, received royal letters of January 22, ordering him to assemble as soon as possible "all those of the three estates of that province who are accustomed to be summoned".[15] The estates were instructed to elect one deputy from each order to attend a meeting of the Estates

---

12   Thomas, *Les Etats provinciaux,* pp. 42-43.
13   Régistres de Poitiers, reg. 32, Sept. 11 and Sept. 21, 1553.
14   For the most recent and thorough treatment of this topic, see J. Russell Major, *The Deputies To The Estates General In Renaissance France* (Madison, 1960), hereafter cited as Major, *The Deputies To The Estates General.*
15   Régistres de Poitiers, reg. 100, Feb. 8, 1649. Also Dr. L. Merle, "Un cahier de doléances d'une paroisse rurale pour les Etats Généraux de 1649: Saint-Christophe-sur-Roc", *Bulletin de la société historique et scientifique des Deux-Sèvres,* IX (1951), 90-91, hereafter cited as Merle, "Un cahier de doleances", *Bul. soc. hist. sc. Deux-Sèvres,* IX.

General to be held in Orleans on March 15. Tudert then fixed the date of the assembly of the three estates of Poitou as February 26, and issued the necessary letters of convocation.

The procedure followed in Poitou from the time the lieutenant general issued the letters of convocation until the three estates of the *sénéchaussée* assembled is not entirely clear. It is evident that it varied considerably from time to time and from place to place.

It became customary in many parts of France during the last half of the sixteenth century to hold preliminary assemblies in the different secondary jurisdictions prior to the meeting of the three estates of the *baillage* or *sénéchaussée*. Each of these local assemblies would prepare a *cahier* or petition of grievances and choose delegates to present it at the *baillage* assembly. As this policy was not called for specifically in the royal instructions, it seems likely that it was instigated by the local royal officials. As will be seen later,[16] the suffrage was greatly extended in some parts of France about this time. In all probability, the motive of the local royal officials in calling for preliminary assemblies was to avoid the confusion of overly large meetings of the three estates of the *baillage*.

One of the most difficult questions to answer is whether or not the first two estates in Poitou participated in preliminary assemblies in the royal secondary jurisdictions. They were certainly instructed to do so in 1649. On this occasion, the letters of convocation were sent from the lieutenant general to royal officials in all of the secondary jurisdictions of Poitou.[17] The officials were instructed to assemble the *three estates* of their jurisdiction and elect one or two delegates from *each order* to attend the meeting of the three estates of the *sénéchaussée*. When the royal officials in the seat of justice of Saint-Maixent received these instructions, they seem to have complied with them. They announced that the three estates of the "siège et ressort" of Saint-Maixent would assemble in that town on February 22 to elect deputies to the meeting of the estates of the *sénéchaussée*.[18]

In connection with this same problem, an interesting case must be considered which occurred in 1614. On June 23 of that year, the bishop of Luçon (later to be known in history as Cardinal Richelieu) was ordered to assemble the three orders of his diocese.[19] He was instructed to see, if

---

16 See below, pp. 105-17.
17 Régistres de Poitiers, reg. 100, Feb. 8, 1649; Merle, "Un cahier de doléances", *Bul. soc. hist. sc. Deux-Sèvres*, IX, 86-91.
18 *Ibid.*
19 Hanotaux, "La Jeunesse de Richelieu, 1585-1614", *Revue des Deux Mondes*, XCIV, 598; Hanotaux, *Histoire du Cardinal de Richelieu*, I, 148.

possible, that one person of each order "of probity, quality and with sufficient and suitable powers for the occasion" be chosen to attend the meeting of the three estates of Poitou. As we shall see later, the diocese and not the royal secondary jurisdiction was the normal unit for preliminary elections of the clergy. It did not usually serve as such for the other two estates, however. This rather unusual procedure may perhaps be explained by the fact that there were no major towns or secondary jurisdictions in the entire diocese of Luçon. Hence, there were no obvious secular divisions to serve as units for preliminary elections and no obvious secular officials to whom the letters of convocation might be sent. As the bishop of Luçon would normally receive the letters of convocation for the clergy of his diocese, it was probably thought convenient to send him those for the other two orders as well and to let the diocese serve as the unit for the preliminary assemblies of the secular estates also. Regardless of the electoral unit, it is clear that in this case, all three orders were instructed to participate in a preliminary assembly to elect delegates to the meeting of the three estates of the *sénéchaussée*. It is the opinion of one historian that this procedure was general in Poitou in 1614 and that each secondary jurisdiction sent two delegates per order to the assembly of the three estates of the *sénéchaussée*.[20]

In 1560 all three orders participated in preliminary elections in at least some of the secondary jurisdictions of Poitou. On Saturday, October 19, 1560, the three estates of the duchy of Châtellerault met to choose delegates and draw up a list of grievances for an assembly of the estates of Poitou.[21] The *procès-verbal* of the assembly of the clergy of Poitou, held as part of the meeting of the three estates of the province on October 28, 1560, indicates that some clergymen attended as the elected representatives of the clergy of various secular jurisdictions.[22] The list of those present includes a representative of the clergy of the barony of Saint-Maixent and a delegate of the clergy of the *châtellenie* of Montreuil-Bonnin.

In spite of all of the above evidence, it is not safe to assume that the nobles and clergy always participated in preliminary assemblies of the secondary jurisdictions. There is no definite proof that the nobles ever actually did, although they were instructed to do so on at least a few

---

[20] Debien, "La question des Etats Généraux de 1649 et de 1651", *B. S. A. O.*, X, 606.
[21] *Lettres du Comte du Lude et autres personnages relatives à l'administration du Poitou de 1559 à 1580*, ed. B. Ledain, *A. H. P.*, XXVII, 35, hereafter cited as *Lettres du Comte du Lude et autres personnages, A. H. P.*, XXVII.
[22] *A. H. P.*, XX, 325-34.

occasions. Unfortunately, the only assembly of the three estates of the *sénéchaussée* during this period for which a complete list of all of the nobles present is available, is that of July 3, 1651.[23] In this case, it is almost certain that the majority of them had not participated in any preliminary assemblies. This is virtually proven by their numbers. Over three hundred attended and hundreds more sent votes by proxy. Not one of them is listed as representing the nobles of any particular region. Moreover, the only conditions for voting at the assembly laid down by the presiding officer were that the person be a noble, residing in Poitou, and eighteen years of age or over. It appears that all such nobles were summoned personally. As will be proven shortly, most members of the clergy who attended meetings of the three estates of Poitou during the period 1560 to 1651 had not been elected in preliminary assemblies of the secular jurisdictions. Indeed, participation by the first two estates in such joint meetings of the three orders of the subordinate jurisdictions of the province seems to have been the exception rather than the general rule.

Let us now examine the more usual procedure by which members of the first two orders were elected or summoned to attend assemblies of the three estates of Poitou at which deputies were to be chosen for meetings of the Estates General. Three ecclesiastical dioceses, Poitiers, Luçon, and Maillezais, corresponded approximately with the *sénéchaussée* of Poitou, and normally provided the framework for preliminary assemblies of the clergy. Presumably the letters of convocation were sent by the lieutenant general to each of the bishops. We have already seen that this was the case in the diocese of Luçon in 1614.[24] The clergy of each diocese then assembled and chose delegates to attend the meeting of the three estates of the *sénéchaussée*. For example, on October 17, 1560, the clergy of the diocese of Luçon met and elected one delegate to represent them at the meeting of the three estates of Poitou to be held on October 28.[25] On October 24, the dioceses of Maillezais and Poitiers each held assemblies and elected delegates for this same meeting.[26] On October 1, 1576 and February 23, 1649, the clergy of the diocese of Poitiers met to elect delegates to attend a meeting of the three estates of the province.[27] As noted several times, the clergy of the diocese of Luçon was summoned to assemble for this purpose in June 1614.

[23]   Mss. de la Bibliothèque de Poitiers, 304 (42).
[24]   See above, pp. 87-88.
[25]   *A. H. P.*, XX, 325-34.
[26]   *Ibid.*
[27]   A. D. Vienne, G 399, Oct. 1, 1576: *Ibid.*, G 411, Feb. 23, 1649.

In addition to those elected by the three diocesan assemblies, other members of the clergy sometimes also attended the meetings of the three estates of Poitou to elect deputies to the Estates General. The possibility that some attended as the elected representatives of the clergy of various secondary royal jurisdictions of Poitou has already been discussed. It is possible also that various members of the regular clergy sometimes attended without having been elected by preliminary diocesan assemblies. That the regular clergy normally participated in meetings of the individual dioceses of Poitou is shown clearly by a number of documents.[28] Yet the *procès-verbal* of the assembly of the clergy of Poitou, held as part of the meeting of the three estates of the province on October 28, 1560, lists the representatives of twelve monasteries and three priories separately and does not include them among those elected at assemblies of the dioceses.[29] This gives the impression that, in this case at least, these various religious communities had been invited to send delegates directly to the assembly of the three estates of the province. The *procès-verbal* of October 28, 1560 also lists separately the representatives of several collegiate churches, a delegate representing the archpriest of Châtellerault and the entire clergy of this archpresbyterate, and the curé of Notre-Dame-la-Grande in Poitiers. Whether they received a personal summons or were elected in an unknown manner, cannot be determined.

In all probability, the bishops of the three dioceses received personal summons. In the *procès-verbal* of October 28, 1560, the vicar-general of the bishop of Poitiers is the first clergyman named. The delegate for the clergy of Maillezais and the delegate for the clergy of Luçon were also declared to be representing the bishops of their respective dioceses.

Very little information is available about the procedure by which the nobles were elected or summoned to the estates of Poitou during this period. Apparently, for the assembly of July 3, 1651, all nobles eighteen years of age and over residing in Poitou, were summoned personally.[30] It is impossible to tell whether or not these same qualifications were required for attendance at earlier meetings. It is quite likely that the majority of nobles who attended such assemblies had received a personal summons. There were some exceptions, however.

The possibility that some nobles were occasionally elected by preliminary assemblies in some of the secondary jurisdictions of Poitou has been discussed already. The mayor and *échevins* of Poitiers provide

---

[28] *Ibid.*, G 399 and G 403; Collection Dom Fonteneau, XII, 469.
[29] *A. H. P.*, XX, 325-34.
[30] See above, p. 89.

another exception to the opinion expressed above that nobles usually received a personal summons. They were *noblesse de cloche,* which meant that they were nobles as long as they held office. In many towns, the *noblesse de cloche* sat with the third estate, but in Poitiers they had won the right to have at least some of their number attend the assemblies of the nobles.[31] Moreover, the mayor claimed the high position of first baron of Poitou and, on some occasions at least, succeeded in taking precedence over all other nobles of the province. Therefore, before each meeting of the three estates, the town council of Poitiers met to select several *échevins* to accompany the mayor to the assembly of the nobles.[32] They chose five *échevins* in 1576 and four in 1588. Royal orders then limited them to two with one vote between them. This was adhered to in 1614 and 1649. However, in 1651, the town council decided that the mayor and all of the *échevins* would attend.[33] They would do so, not as the representatives of the town council, but as individual nobles. It was felt that their presence would insure that the mayor would be given precedence over all the other nobles "as first baron of Poitou, just as had been the case at the assemblies of the estates held in the years 1614 and 1649".

Thanks to more abundant information, the preliminary elections of the third estate in Poitou can be described more clearly. Usually they were conducted in two stages. Each parish elected delegates to an assembly of the third estate of the secondary jurisdiction which, in turn, chose deputies to attend the meeting of the three estates of the *sénéchaussée.* The letters of convocation were distributed in the opposite order, from the lieutenant-general of Poitou to each secondary jurisdiction, and then from the royal officials in each secondary jurisdiction to every parish. The procedure followed in the principal towns was somewhat different and will be described later.

Let us examine, for example, the procedure followed in 1649. The lieutenant general of Poitou sent letters of convocation to all of the secondary jurisdictions of the province.[34] The royal officials in each of these areas then set a date for an assembly of the three estates of their

---

[31] For disputes over this right and for the royal decision settling the issue, see below, pp. 126-27.

[32] Régistres de Poitiers, reg. 42, Sep. 30, 1576; *Ibid.,* reg. 48, Aug. 22, 1588; *Ibid.,* reg. 69, Aug. 19, 1614; *Ibid.,* reg. 100, Feb. 22 and Feb. 26, 1649; *Ibid.,* reg. 102, June 29 and July 3, 1651.

[33] *Ibid.,* reg. 102, June 29 and July 3, 1651.

[34] *Ibid.,* reg. 100, Feb. 8, 1649; Merle, "Un cahier de doléances", *Bul. soc. hist. sc. Deux-Sèvres,* **IX,** 86-91.

jurisdiction.[35] This assembly was announced "to the sound of the trumpet and public cry" in the chief town, and the letters of convocation were read at mass the following Sunday in every church in town. The royal officials also wrote to every parish and village in their entire jurisdiction instructing them to elect one or two delegates to bring their list of grievances to the assembly. To each of these letters they attached a copy of the lieutenant-general's letter of summons to the provincial assembly. Their instructions were read at mass the following Sunday in each parish, and then posted on the church door. A meeting of the inhabitants of the parish was then held to draw up a list of grievances and elect delegates to take it to the assembly of the secondary jurisdiction.

The *procès-verbal* of the assembly held in Saint-Christophe-sur-Roc, a parish of ninety hearths in the secondary jurisdiction of Saint-Maixent, on February 21, 1649 has survived.[36] As such *procès-verbaux* from rural parishes are rare, the procedure described is of considerable interest. The time of the meeting was indicated by the ringing of the church bell, and the inhabitants of the parish assembled outside the church door. Pierre Pillet, notary and *procureur-syndic* of the parish, presided. He announced that he had received a copy of a letter of summons of the lieutenant general, dated February 6. Attached to it was another letter from the royal officials of the seat of justice of Saint-Maixent, dated February 13. This second letter stated that the three estates of the "siège et ressort" of Saint-Maixent would assemble in that town in the palace of justice on February 22, to elect deputies to the meeting of the estates of the province. The parish of Saint-Christophe-sur-Roc was invited to send one or two delegates to the assembly in Saint-Maixent.

The *procès-verbal* then lists the names of those who attended the parish assembly. Twenty-nine men are named and several others also attended. It was stated that they constituted "the largest and wisest portion of the said inhabitants of the said parish". They chose the parish priest, Louis Ribard, to represent them at the assembly in Saint-Maixent and present their grievances, which are listed. Although a priest, he presumably sat with the third estate. The *procès-verbal* was signed by Ribard, Pillot the notary and presiding officer, and two others. To it was attached the letter of summons from the lieutenant-general and the

---

[35] Even although, in this case, all three estates were instructed to participate in the assembly, this would have very little effect on the procedure followed by the third estate, as it is probable that the three orders would choose their delegates separately, just as they did at meetings of the three estates of the *sénéchaussée*.

[36] Merle, "Un cahier de doléances", *Bul. soc. hist. sc. Deux-Sèvres*, IX, 86-91.

letter from the royal officials in Saint-Maixent. Brief reference to preliminary assemblies in the parishes of Pouzauges and Mouilleron in the diocese of Luçon in October 1560,[37] and in each parish of the diocese of Luçon on August 10, 1614 [38] indicate that such assemblies were usually the first stage in the election of deputies for the third estate.

The next stage was normally the assembly of the secondary jurisdiction. This was called for in February 1649 in the letters of convocation issued by the lieutenant-general of Poitou.[39] At these meetings, one or two delegates were to be elected from the third estate to attend the assembly in Poitiers "with powers, instructions, and lists of grievances (*mémoires*)". [40] In 1649, the assembly for the secondary jurisdiction of Saint-Maixent was scheduled for February 22,[41] while the meeting of the secondary *sénéchaussée* of Montmorillon took place on February 19.[42] At the latter assembly, two delegates for the third estate were chosen to attend the meeting of the estates of Poitou.

Some information on such secondary assemblies in other years is available. On Saturday, October 19, 1560, the three estates of the Duchy of Châtellerault met to choose delegates and draw up a list of grievances for an assembly of the three estates of Poitou.[43] Another document describes an assembly of the third estate of the town and *élection* of Saint-Maixent to draw up a list of grievances to be presented at a meeting of the estates of Poitou.[44] This assembly in Saint-Maixent was probably held in August 1588. As seen above,[45] the diocese of Luçon probably served in lieu of a secondary jurisdiction for elections of the third estate in 1614. Perhaps it did in other years as well, due to the lack of towns and royal seats of justice in this region of Lower Poitou.

[37] A. H. P., XXVII, 36.
[38] Hanotaux, *Histoire du Cardinal de Richelieu*, I, 149; Hanotaux, "La Jeunesse de Richelieu", *Revue des Deux Mondes*, XCIV, 599.
[39] As noted before, in this case, the instructions called for an assembly of the *three estates* of each secondary jurisdiction. Régistres de Poitiers, reg. 100, Feb. 8, 1649; Merle, "Un cahier de doléances", *Bul. soc. hist. sc. Deux-Sèvres*, IX, 86 and 90.
[40] *Ibid.*, 90.
[41] *Ibid.*, 91.
[42] *Journal de M. Demaillasson, A. H. P.*, XXXVI, 6.
[43] *Lettres du Comte du Lude et autres personnages, A. H. P.*, XXVII, 35.
[44] Collection Dom Fonteneau, XL, 54, pub. *A. H. P.*, XX, 381-82. The beginning and the ending of the document are missing. From too hasty a reading, Dom Fonteneau dated it incorrectly as 1559. This date is mentioned in the document and apparently caught his eye, but it was not stated to be the date of the assembly. Internal evidence dates it almost conclusively as August 1588.
[45] See above, pp. 87-88.

In addition to the representatives of the third estate elected in each subordinate jurisdiction, certain towns had the traditional right to choose delegates directly to attend the meeting of the three estates of the *séné-chaussée*.[46] The procedure in the town of Poitiers is described clearly in several documents.[47] The lieutenant-general of Poitou instructed the mayor of Poitiers to invite the "procureurs et fabriqueurs" of the twenty-six parishes of the town to elect one or two deputies each to attend the assembly of the third estate of the province. The *procureurs* and *fabriqueurs* were to announce the coming assembly of the estates of Poitou at the end of mass the following Sunday. Then, usually on the Sunday following the announcement, the bells in all of the churches of Poitiers would be rung, and the "manans et habitans" of each parish would assemble to elect their delegates.

The town council of Poitiers always chose special delegates to represent it at the assembly of the third estate of the province.[48] They normally chose two delegates, but on September 30, 1576 they chose four. These men would attend the meeting of the third estate of the *sénéchaussée* in addition to the delegates elected by the twenty-six parishes of Poitiers.

The town council of Poitiers seems to have played a leading role in deciding the procedure to be followed in drawing up the town's *cahier* of grievances. At a meeting of the council on August 22, 1588, it was decided that a box would be placed in the church of the Jacobins in which anyone could deposit his complaints.[49] The mayor and the two delegates chosen by the town council to attend the meeting of the third estate of the province would collect them and consider them in preparing the *cahier*.

Several other towns in Poitou also had the right to choose deputies directly to attend the assembly of the third estate of the province without participating in the elections of the secondary jurisdictions. In August 1614, the town of Niort was invited to send delegates to the assembly of the third estate of Poitou to be held the following Tuesday.[50]

[46]   Olivier-Martin, *Histoire du droit français*, pp. 370-71.
[47]   Régistres de Poitiers, reg. 42, Sep. 17 and Sep. 30, 1576; *Ibid.*, reg. 48, Aug. 18, and Aug. 22, 1588; *Extrait des mémoires de René de Brilhac, Sire du Parc*, ed. B. Ledain, *A.H.P.*, XV, 10-49, hereafter cited as *Mémoires de René de Brilhac, A.H.P.*, XV; Thibaudeau, *Histoire du Poitou*, III, 204-05.
[48]   Régistres de Poitiers, reg. 42, Sept. 30, 1576; *Ibid.*, reg. 48, Aug. 22, 1588; *Ibid.*, reg. 69, Aug. 18, 1614; *Ibid.*, reg. 100, Feb. 22, 1649; *Ibid.*, reg. 102, July 3, 1651.
[49]   *Ibid.*, reg. 48, Aug. 22, 1588.
[50]   L. Favre, *Histoire de la ville de Niort depuis son origine jusqu'en 1789* (Niort,

Accordingly, the mayor of Niort summoned the *échevins* and inhabitants to meet and elect three delegates from each parish of the town. The meeting was properly announced "by the usual means", but was very poorly attended. The mayor waited from 1 P.M. to 3 P.M., and then called off the meeting because only five people were present. On this occasion, Niort probably sent no delegates at all to the assembly of the estates of Poitou unless they were chosen by the town council.

Also in August 1614, the town of Saint-Maixent was invited to send one or two delegates to the meeting of the three estates of the province.[51] The town council decided not to call an assembly of the inhabitants as the town had no specific grievances, merely general ones which they felt would appear in other *cahiers*. Probably then, they sent no delegates to this assembly of the estates of Poitou.

As a rule, the delegates from each order of the entire province did not assemble until the appointed day of the joint meeting of the three estates of Poitou. In 1614, however, they each held preliminary assemblies. On August 12, nine days before the three estates were scheduled to meet, separate assemblies were held of the clergy, nobles, and the third estate of Poitou.[52] The third estate met again on August 19.[53] At the first of these two meetings, they chose twelve of their number to prepare their *cahier*. The second meeting was probably held to discuss its progress. Almost undoubtedly, the purpose of the assemblies of the clergy and the nobles on August 12 was to begin the preparation of their respective *cahiers* too.

B. PRESIDING OFFICERS

The type of presiding officers at meetings of the three estates of Poitou varied somewhat, but prior to about 1470, they were normally specially

1880), pp. 233-34. Favre dates this assembly in Niort as September 7, 1614. It seems more likely that it was held August 7, as the third estate of the province met on Tuesday, August 12.

[51] *Archives de Saint-Maixent*, B.B.2, *Inventaire-Sommaire des archives communales antérieures à 1790 de Saint-Maixent*, ed. A. Richard (Paris, 1863); A. Richard, "Recherches sur l'organisation communale de la ville de Saint-Maixent jusqu'en 1790", *M. S. A. O.*, ser, 1, XXXIV (1869), 360, hereafter cited as Richard, "Recherches sur l'organisation communale de Saint-Maixent", *M. S. A. O.*, ser. 1, XXXIV.

[52] Hanotaux, *Histoire du Cardinal de Richelieu*, I, 149; Hanotaux, "La Jeunesse de Richelieu", *Revue des Deux-Mondes*, XCIV, 599; *Mémoires de René de Brilhac*, *A. H. P.*, XV, 10-49; Thibaudeau, *Histoire du Poitou*, III, 204-05.

[53] Régistres de Poitiers, reg. 69, Aug. 18, 1614.

appointed commissioners. As a rule, these commissioners were from two to four in number,[54] although, on a few occasions, only one man seems to have been entrusted with the task.[55] Various types of men were chosen. The duke of Berry generally appointed his own officials, as in September 1412, when all four commissioners were ducal councillors.[56] One of them, Guillaume Taveau, was also the duke's chamberlain. Taveau, incidentally, had also served as a commissioner in 1390.[57] Charles VII, as count of Poitou (1416-22), and as king after 1422, usually appointed one bishop to the commission. The bishop did not necessarily come from Poitou. In November 1416, Charles chose the bishop of Clermont,[58] and in December 1423, he named Hugh de Combarel, bishop of Béziers.[59] The latter became bishop of Poitiers in 1424, and was appointed one of the commissioners to assemble the three estates of Poitou in November of that year and again in 1435.[60] Usually Charles also chose a great noble from Poitou as one of the commissioners. The viscount of Thouars was named in November 1416 and November 1424.[61] Jean de Torsay, Grand Master of Crossbowmen of France, and one of the leading nobles of Poitou, was named in December 1423 and November 1424.[62] Frequently a royal official was chosen, such as Nicolas de la Barre, Councillor and *Maître des Requêtes* of the king's household, in December 1423.[63] Occasionally a leading citizen of

[54] Two in November 1390; three on December 16, 1423 and November 1, 1424; four in November 1416 and in 1435.

[55] Bernard d'Armagnac, lieutenant-general for the dauphin between the Loire and the Dordogne, on November 25, 1421; A. Thomas, "Nouveau documents sur les Etats provinciaux de la Haute Marche (1418-1446)", *Annales du Midi*, XXV (1913), 441, hereafter cited as Thomas, "Nouveau documents", *Annales du Midi*, XXV. The seigneur de Belleville in September 1461. He was acting as a royal commissioner in Poitou at the time to receive oaths of loyalty to the new king, Louis XI; Régistres de Poitiers, reg. 4, fol. 91, September 25, 1461; A. C. Poitiers, J 1277.

[56] Lacour, "Une incursion angalise", *A. H. P.*, XLVIII, 1-87.

[57] Fillon, ed., *Documents pour servir à l'histoire du Bas Poitou*, I.

[58] A. C. Poitiers, J 546-47.

[59] B. N., p.o. vol. 1612: Labbé, doss. 37,421, no. 3, and Abbé L. Niel, "Histoire des Evêques de Tulle. Hugues de Combarel, XIIIe Evêque", *Bulletin de la société des lettres, sciences et arts de la Corrèze*, X (1888), 53, hereafter cited as Niel, "Histoire des Evêques de Tulle", *Bul. soc. lettres, sciences, arts Corrèze*, X.

[60] B. N., p.o. vol. 247: Beaumont, doss. 5423, no. 3; *Ibid.*, vol. 1612: Labbé, doss. 37,421, no. 4; *Ibid.*, vol. 2855; Torsay, doss. 63,456, no. 13; *Ibid.*, ms. fr. 25,969, no. 956.

[61] A. C. Poitiers, J 546-547;B. N., p.o. vol. 247; Beaumont, doss. 5423, no. 3; *Ibid.*, vol. 1612: Labbé, doss. 37,421, no. 4.

[62] *Ibid.*, vol. 1612: Labbé, doss. 37,421, no. 3; *Ibid.*, vol. 247: Beaumont, doss. 5423, no. 3; *Ibid.*, vol. 2855: Torsay, doss. 63,456, no. 13.

[63] *Ibid.*, vol. 201: La Barre, no. 9.

the town of Poitiers was selected, such as Maurice Claveurier in 1435.[64]

Between about 1470 and 1559, the type of presiding officers varied. Sometimes they were local royal officials, such as the seneschal or the lieutenant-general of Poitou. Sometimes they were specially appointed royal commissioners. They were usually from two to four in number.

On the three occasions when the estates of Poitou met to ratify treaties, the presiding officers were local royal officials. Jean Chambon, *maître des requêtes* and royal lieutenant presided in c. December 1482; André de Vivonne, seigneur de la Chasteignerai, seneschal of Poitou, in March 1497; François de la Trémoïlle, royal lieutenant in Poitou and Saintonge, and François Doyneau, lieutenant general of the *sénéchaussée* of Poitou in November 1529.[65] The presiding officers at the assembly of c. December 1483 to elect deputies to the Estates General cannot be determined.

At the two meetings to codify the custom, specially appointed royal commissioners presided. In both cases, all of them were advocates in the Parlement of Paris and were headed by a President in Parlement. Obviously, the nature of these assemblies made necessary a special type of presiding officer. In October 1514, two royal commissioners presided, headed by Thibault Baillet, President in the Parlement of Paris.[66] In October 1559, three royal commissioners presided, headed by Christofle de Thou, President in the Parlement of Paris.[67]

Supervision of the different assemblies held between 1549 and 1553 regarding the salt taxes was sometimes entrusted to royal commissioners and sometimes to local royal officials. On July 11, 1549 and October 1, 1553, royal commissioners officiated, four in the first case and three in the second.[68] At one meeting in November 1549, the royal lieutenant-general of Poitou apparently presided.[69] At the assembly of September 25, 1553, one document states that royal commissioners would officiate,[70] while another source indicates that the seneschal or his lieutenant would fulfil this responsibility.[71]

The presiding officers at meetings of the estates of Poitou between

---

[64] *Ibid.*, ms. fr. 25,969, no. 956.
[65] A. C. Poitiers, M, reg. 11, fol. 1 r⁰; Rymer, V, part 2, 91; Bouchet, p. 453; B. N., ms. fr. 20,084, p. 57.
[66] Bourdot de Richebourg, IV, 747-74.
[67] *Ibid.*, 818.
[68] Bouchet, p. 574; Régistres de Poitiers, reg. 32, Sep. 4 and Sep. 21, 1553; A. C. Poitiers, C 33.
[69] Régistres de Poitiers, reg. 31, Nov. 5, 1549.
[70] *Ibid.*, reg. 32, Sep. 11, 1553.
[71] *Ibid.*, Sep. 21, 1553.

1560 and 1651 were always local royal officials. They were from one to five in number, and usually included a royal advocate. In October 1560 they consisted of the seneschal, his lieutenant, and a royal advocate in Poitiers.[72] In August 1588 the assembly was held "in the presence of the seneschal".[73] Whether he was the only presiding officer or not cannot be determined. In August 1614 the assessor, "in the absence of the lieutenant-general", and a royal advocate were in charge of the assembly.[74] In February 1649 this role was filled by the lieutenant-general and a royal advocate.[75] In July 1651 there were five presiding officers, headed by Martin Reveau, particular lieutenant and civil assessor in Poitiers.[76] All of the other four were either royal advocates or *procureurs royaux* at the seat of justice of Poitiers.

C. LOCATION AND LENGTH OF ASSEMBLIES

The location of the assemblies of the three estates of Poitou during the period prior to about 1470 varied considerably. Only about half of them were held in Poitiers. Most of the others were held in five other towns of the province, but on two occasions, the meetings took place outside Poitou. Of the twenty-six assemblies of the three estates of Poitou meeting alone for which the location can be determined during these years, thirteen were held in Poitiers, four in Niort, three in Bressuire, two in Thouars, one in Saint-Loup and one in Saint-Maixent. The two meetings outside the province took place in June 1417 at Saumur [77] and September 1430 at Chinon.[78] In addition, eight joint meetings were held with the estates of other provinces. Four of these assemblies were held in Poitou (two at Niort, one at Saint-Maixent, and one at Poitiers). Of the other four meetings, two were held at Tours, one at Saumur and one at Limoges. An assembly of the barons of Poitou was held at Niort.[79]

---

[72]   *A. H. P.*, XX, 325-34.
[73]   Collection Dom Fonteneau, LX, 457.
[74]   *Mémoires de René de Brilhac, A. H. P.*, XV, 10-49.
[75]   Régistres de Poitiers, reg. 100, March 1, 1649.
[76]   *Ibid.*, reg. 102, July 3, 1651; Mss. de la Bibliothèque de Poitiers, 304 (42).
[77]   A. C. Poitiers, J 554. The fact that the dauphin presided in person may perhaps explain why they met outside the province. The dauphin happened to be in Saumur and summoned them to come to him.
[78]   A. Thomas, "Les Etats Généraux sous Charles VII", *Revue Historique*, XL (1889), 70. There is no obvious explanation as to why this assembly was held outside the province, unless perhaps it was a joint meeting with the estates of several other provinces.
[79]   Ledain, "Maires de Poitiers", p. 355; Régistres de Poitiers, reg. 2, fol. 90.

On only three occasions during this period is the precise building in which the assembly took place specified. In November 1447 the three estates met in the town hall of Poitiers.[80] On August 9, 1461 and August 20,1466, they met in the palace of the counts in Poitiers.[81]

After about 1470 the three estates of Poitou normally met in Poitiers. In fact, the only known exception was the meeting in November 1529, which was held in Lusignan.[82] The precise building in which they met varied until the mid-sixteenth century. In c. December 1482, September1553, and October 1559, they met in the royal palace of justice in Poitiers.[83] In October 1514 they assembled in the refectory of the convent of the Friars Minor.[84] In July 1549 they met with the estates of neighbouring provinces in the bishop's palace in Poitiers.[85] Beginning in 1560, however, every assembly of the three estates of the province was held in the royal palace of justice in Poitiers.

In 1560 and at each subsequent meeting, the three orders then met separately to elect their deputies and prepare their *cahiers*.[86] The location of the assemblies of the clergy varied.[87] In 1560 they met in the episcopal palace; in 1576 in the chapter hall of the cathedral of Poitiers; in 1614 in the council hall of the palace of justice; in 1649 in the assembly room of the council (probably the same room as in 1614); and in 1651 in the chapel of the palace of justice. The location of the assemblies of the nobles also varied. On August 21, and August 24, 1614 they met in the chapel of the palace of justice.[88] In February 1649 they met in the

---

[80] B. N., ms. fr. 20,084, p. 43.

[81] Régistres de Poitiers, reg. 4, fol. 91. *Ibid.*, reg. 6, Aug. 2-27, 1466. Much of this fine example of late fourteenth century civil architecture still stands, including the great hall where the meeting was probably held. It is today part of the Palais de Justice in Poitiers.

[82] Bouchet, p. 453; B. N., ms. fr. 20,084, p. 57. It is also possible that delegates from Poitou attended an assembly of estates outside the province at Tarbes on April 28, 1549. See *A. H. P.*, IV, 314-15.

[83] A. C. Poitiers, M, reg. 11, fol. 1, r⁰; Ledain, "Maires de Poitiers", p. 468; Régistres de Poitiers, reg. 32, Sep. 18 and Sep. 23, 1553; Bourdot de Richebourg, IV, 818.

[84] *Ibid.*, 743.

[85] *Documents inédits pour servir à l'histoire du Poitou, publiés par la Société des Antiquaires de l'Ouest*, pp. 157-58, hereafter cited as *Documents inédits pour l'histoire du Poitou*.

[86] The general question of whether or not the three orders normally met together or separately in Poitou will be discussed fully in section F of this chapter.

[87] *A. H. P.*, XX, 325-34; A. D. Vienne, G 399, October 1 and October 17, 1576; *Ibid.*, G 411, Feb. 26, 1649; *Ibid.*, July 3, 1651.

[88] Mémoires de René de Brilhac, *A. H. P.*, XV, 10-49; Hanotaux, "La Jeunesse de Richelieu", *Revue des Deux Mondes*, XCIV, 600; Hanotaux, *Histoire du Cardinal de Richelieu*, I, 150.

"chambre du bureau".[89] In July 1651, because of their large number, they assembled in the convent of the Cordeliers.[90] The delegates from the third estate always remained in the main assembly hall of the palace of justice where the opening joint session of the three orders had been held. When the clergymen and nobles had withdrawn, they proceeded with the election of their deputies and the preparation of their *cahier*.

The meetings of the three estates of Poitou were fairly brief. Those held prior to 1560 varied in length from one to about five days. Frequently they lasted for only one day, as on March 28, 1497. The joint session with the estates of several neighbouring provinces which started on May 1, 1426, lasted three days and the assembly of December 1425 lasted for four days. Probably the two longest meetings during this period were those held from November 17, to November 22, 1416, and from October 16, to October 21, 1559. The length of the former can be accounted for by the fact that the complicated matter of negotiations with the turbulent Jean L'Archevêque, seigneur of Parthenay, was being discussed. At the meeting of October 1559 the task of recodifying the customs of the province proved to be quite lengthy.

After about 1560, as we have seen, the three estates of Poitou met together in a brief opening session and then separated to elect their deputies to the Estates General and prepare their *cahiers* of grievances. As a rule, the joint opening assembly lasted only a few hours. The separate meetings of the three orders varied considerably in length. The assembly of the third estate in February 1649 lasted only one day. The deputies from Montmorillon left for Poitiers on February 25, attended the meeting on February 26, and returned home on February 27.[91] The assembly of the nobles in 1651 began on July 3 and finished the following morning.[92] The clergy sometimes required a number of meetings to complete its *cahiers* as in 1614.[93] The whole procedure in October 1576 was more lengthy than usual. Between October 1, and October 17, each order appears to have met several times and there were at least three joint assemblies of the three estates.[94] In other years,

[89] Régistres de Poitiers, reg. 100, March 1, 1649. It is difficult to identify this room exactly.

[90] *Ibid.*, reg. 102, July 3, 1651. Also Mss. de la Bibliothèque de Poitiers, 304 (42).

[91] *Journal de M. Demaillasson, A. H. P.*, XXXVI, 6-7.

[92] Régistres de Poitiers, reg. 102, July 3, 1651; Mss. de la Bibliothèque de Poitiers, 304 (42).

[93] Lacroix, "Richelieu à Luçon", *M. S. A. O.*, XII, 283; Hanotaux, "La Jeunesse de Richelieu", *Revue des Deux Mondes*, XCIV, 600-601; Hanotaux, *Histoire du Cardinal de Richelieu*, I, 150.

[94] Régistres de Poitiers, reg. 42, September 17, September 24, and September 30,

however, each order completed its *cahier* more rapidly and the three estates did not normally hold any further joint meetings after the opening session.

D. COMPOSITION

One of the chief points to emerge from a study of the composition of assemblies of the estates of Poitou is that a notable increase occurred in the size of these meetings about the middle of the sixteenth century as a result of an extension of the suffrage. The two chief questions to be examined then are whether or not this led to a permanent extension in representation and why the marked increase in the number of deputies attending these meetings occurred in the first place. The first question can be answered with a fair degree of certainty, but the evidence is insufficient to provide a very definite solution to the second.

Very little information is available on the precise composition of the three estates of Poitou before the sixteenth century except for references concerning the delegates from the town of Poitiers. The only nobleman whose presence at a fifteenth century assembly can be attested definitely was constable Richemont who attended the meeting of November 1447 as seigneur of Parthenay.[95] None of the names of representatives of the first estate during this period are known. At the assembly of March 28, 1497, the clergy and nobles, or their proctors, attended "in large numbers", but none of their names can be determined.[96]

As far as the third estate is concerned, the representation during the fifteenth century seems to have been limited to the deputies of a few of the chief towns. The only meetings for which any specific information is available for towns other than Poitiers are those of November 1447 and March 28, 1497. In the first case, Niort was represented.[97] Parthenay was also invited to send deputies, but whether it actually did so cannot be determined.[98] On March 28, 1497, the deputies from the third estate

---

1576; A. D. Vienne, G 399, October 1, and October 17, 1576; *Journal de Guillaume et Michel le Riche, avocats du Roi à Saint-Maixent*, ed. A. de la Fontenelle de Vaudoré (Saint-Maixent, 1846), October 6, 1576, hereafter cited as *Journal de Guillaume et Michel le Riche; Lettres adressées à Jean et Guy de Daillon, Comtes du Lude*, ed. B. Ledain, *A. H. P.*, XIV, 78, hereafter cited as *Lettres à Jean et Guy de Daillon, A. H. P.*, XIV.

[95] Ledain, *La Gâtine historique et monumentale*, pp. 217-18.

[96] Rymer, V, part 2, 91.

[97] B. N., ms. fr., 20,084, p. 43.

[98] Ledain, *La Gâtine historique et monumentale*, pp. 217-18.

included the mayor, *échevins*, and bourgeois of Poitiers, Niort, Fontenay-le-Comte, and Saint-Maixent.[99] The towns of Thouars, Parthenay, Châtellerault, "and other places" were also represented. On several other occasions, it was stated that invitations were sent to various towns in Poitou, but they were not named. In all probability, they included most of those represented at the assembly of March 1497.

The valuable town archives of Poitiers provides considerable information about the deputies from that town to meetings of the three estates of the province. Down to at least 1470, they were always chosen by the town council and were usually from two to four in number.[100] As a rule they were selected from the twelve *échevins* and the mayor. On six out of the thirteen occasions for which information is available, the mayor was chosen. Occasionally, however, some notable figure was selected who was neither mayor nor *échevin*, such as Adam de Cambray, president of the Parlement of Poitiers, in December 1425.[101] The town chose the same man frequently to represent them. Jean Guichard was a delegate in November 1416, June 1417, December 1425, and March 1428.[102] Jean Larcher served in November 1416, June 1417, and October 1418.[103] Maurice Claveurier was a deputy in June 1417 and October 1418.[104] Herbert Taunay was chosen in June 1417, October 1418, and March 1428.[105] All of these men served as mayor of Poitiers at least once; Claveurier on several occasions.

The first assembly of the estates of Poitou for which a reasonably complete list of those present is available is the meeting of October 16, 1514 for the codification of the custom laws of the province.[106] Due to the nature of this assembly, the type of men present was probably not typical as most of them were lawyers. However, the people and places they represented probably were typical. Unfortunately, the royal letters of convocation, specifying who was to be summoned, have not survived.

---

[99]   Rymer, V, part 2, 91.
[100] Two in December 1412, November 1416, March 1428, August 1440, and 1450; three in October 1418, December 1425, and September 1461; four in June 1417 and January 1446. In November 1446 it was decided that six specified men "or any three of them" would attend.
[101] Régistres de Poitiers, reg. 2, fol. 72. Also Ledain, "Maires de Poitiers", pp. 348-49.
[102] A. C. Poitiers, J 546-547 and J 554; Régistres de Poitiers, reg. 2, fols. 72 and 90.
[103] A. C. Poitiers, J 546-547 and J 554; Régistres de Poitiers, reg. 1, fols. 129-130.
[104] A. C. Poitiers, J 554; Régistres de Poitiers, reg. 1. fols. 129-130.
[105] Régistres de Poitiers, reg. 1, fols. 129-130; *Ibid.*, reg. 2, fol. 90; A. C. Poitiers, J 554.
[106] Bourdot de Richebourg, IV, 743-74.

However, the letters of convocation for the neighbouring provinces of Touraine and Saintonge for the codification of customs, in 1507 and 1520 respectively, have been preserved.[107] In both cases, the royal instructions stated that the prelates, abbots and chapters should be summoned for the clergy, and the counts, barons, *châtellains*, and seigneurs with high justice for the nobles. For the third estate the instructions were somewhat less specific, stating merely that royal officials, advocates, "practitioners, and other good and notable bourgeois" should be summoned. As these instructions were identical for Touraine and Saintonge, it is reasonable to assume that they were probably the same for Poitou. Let us examine the composition of the assembly of the three estates of Poitou on October 16, 1514, to attempt to see if this was the case.

All told, about seventy deputies attended this meeting, including about twenty representatives of the first estate, about thirty representatives of the nobles, and about twenty delegates from the third estate. The delegates for the first estate were: the vicar-general of the bishop of Poitiers, ten abbots, and proctors for the dean, canons, and chapter of Saint-Hilaire-le-Grand of Poitiers, the canons and chapter of Notre-Dame-la-Grande of Poitiers, the bishop, monks and chapter of Maillezais, and the deans, canons, and chapter of the Cathedral of Luçon, whose episcopal seat was vacant. The deputies for the nobles included a number of proctors for the king, the lady of Angoulême, the prince of La Roche-sur-Yon, the duke of Longueville, and Louis de Graville, admiral of France, for various baronies and seigneuries which they held in Poitou. Also present for the second estate were the seneschal of Poitou, a seneschal and the lieutenant of a bailiff from two secondary *sénéchaussées,* and *baillages* of the province, seven viscounts, barons, *châtellains,* or their proctors, and ten seigneurs. The deputies for the third estate were: the lieutenant-general of Poitiers, the mayor of Poitiers, the conservator of royal privileges of the University of Poitiers, three other delegates from Poitiers, and a number of delegates from Niort, Fontenay-le-Comte, Montmorillon, and Lusignan. Every deputy for the third estate was either a royal official or a lawyer. In addition to all of the above, it was stated that several other clergymen, nobles and "practitioners" were present.

As nearly as can be ascertained, all of the above deputies of each order were of the type specified in the royal instructions to Touraine and Saintonge. The deputies from the clergy were all bishops and abbots,

---

[107] *Ibid.,* 599-600, and 864.

or their representatives, and delegates from various chapters. No parish priests were present. If the ten seigneurs who attended had powers of high justice, all of the nobles were of the type specified. All of the deputies for the third estate might be described as "royal officials, advocates, practitioners and notable bourgeois". No deputies were present from the villages or country parishes.

After examining the composition of meetings down to and including that of 1514, it is evident that representation at assemblies of the three estates of Poitou during the fifteenth and early sixteenth centuries was rather restricted. There is no reason to believe that it was any more extensive for the first two estates during the fifteenth century than it was in 1514. Although the number who actually attended undoubtedly varied considerably, the summons probably was restricted to bishops, abbots, and chapters for the clergy, and counts, viscounts, barons, *châtellains* and seigneurs with high justice for the nobles. Representation for the third estate was clearly limited to the chief towns. Poitiers normally sent from two to four delegates. There were only six or seven other towns of any consequence in the province. If all of them sent one or two deputies each, and even allowing for the possible presence of a few royal officials, it is probably safe to guess that the deputies from the third estate did not normally exceed twenty or twenty-five in number.

Although information about the composition of assemblies of the three estates of Poitou between 1514 and 1559 is too limited to permit certainty, there is nothing to indicate any great extension in the representation. Very little is known about the deputies present at the meeting of November 27, 1529 for the ratification of the Treaties of Madrid and Cambrai. One source states that deputies attended from each order and town.[108] Poitiers was represented by two delegates. The royal letters patent authorizing the assembly of the estates of Poitou, and other provinces, on July 11, 1549, called for each town to elect three deputies, one from each estate.[109] The town of Poitiers elected Philippe Chambon, abbot of Notre-Dame for the clergy, François Doyneau, royal lieutenant-general of Poitou for the nobles, and Jean Pellison for the third estate. Doyneau requested to be relieved of the task because he was a royal official and felt that he could better further the interests of the town in that capacity alone. He was persuaded to accept, however. This policy for each town to elect one deputy for each estate is rather unusual. There is nothing to suggest that it was followed for any other meeting of the estates of Poi-

---

[108]   B. N., ms. fr. 20,084, p. 57. Bouchet, p. 453.
[109]   Régistres de Poitiers, reg. 30, July 6, 1549.

tou during this period. Whether the nobles and clergy outside the town were summoned as usual cannot be determined. The only information available about the composition of the meeting of September 25, 1553 concerns the town and *châtellenie* of Poitiers.[110] The mayor, *échevins,* and bourgeois of the town were invited to attend or elect deputies. They chose four of their number including the mayor, to represent them. The town council then summoned the inhabitants of the parishes of the town and *châtellenie* of Poitiers to elect deputies. It is possible then that the representation from the town of Poitiers was somewhat larger than at previous meetings, and it seems to have been extended to include the entire *châtellenie.*[111] At none of these meetings is there anything to indicate that villages, country parishes, and parish priests were represented.

An extension of representation is definitely shown by the assembly of October 16-21, 1559 for the recodification of the customs of Poitou. An extensive list of those present has been preserved in the *procès-verbal* of this meeting.[112] The deputies for the clergy included a number of proctors representing the bishop of Poitiers, the prior, canons, and chapter of Maillezais, and the bishop, dean, chapter and canons of Luçon. Also present were representatives of the dean, canons, and cathedral chapter of Poitiers, and the canons and chapter of Saint Hilaire-le-Grand of Poitiers. The bishop of Maillezais attended in person. The *procès-verbal* then lists various abbots, or their proctors representing the different monasteries of Poitou. In each case they were assisted by a lawyer. Then are listed the representatives of various royal and collegiate churches and priories. A number of convents for women were represented by proctors, most of whom were lawyers. Finally, six parish priests, or their representatives, were present.

The delegates for the second estate included several proctors, assisted by lawyers, representing the duke of Longueville, the prince of La Roche-sur-Yon, the duchess of Montpensier, and her son Louis de Bourbon, for their holdings in Poitou. Then follows a long list of nobles, most of them represented by proctors. A few nobles appeared in person, such as Georges de la Trémoïlle, for his barony of Olonne, and his *seigneurie*

---

[110] *Ibid.,* reg. 32, Sept. 11 and Sept. 21, 1553.
[111] At the beginning of the fifteenth century, the *châtellenie* of Poitiers was by far the most extensive of the eleven *châtellenies* in the county of Poitou. It included such relatively distant and scattered areas as the viscounty of Thouars and the island of Yeu. See Lacour, *Le Gouvernement de Jean, Duc de Berry,* pp. 131-32. Whether it had been subdivided by 1553 is difficult to determine, but it is probably safe to assume that it still included more than the town of Poitiers and its immediate suburbs.
[112] Bourdot de Richebourg, IV, 818-23.

of Gençay. It is interesting to note that this same man was listed among the deputies for the clergy as abbot of Saint Laon de Thouars and Notre-Dame de Chambon. Two nobles appeared, not only for themselves, but for the entire nobility of the duchy of Châtellerault, by whom they had been commissioned. Several nobles of the robe, entitled "Maître", but lords of various seigneuries, are listed with the nobles, and many of them were present in person. Some of this latter group were counsellors in the Parlement of Paris.

Next follows a list of royal officials and "practitioners", who were presumably considered to be members of the third estate. They included the lieutenant-general and the criminal judge of the *sénéchaussée* of Poitou, the *lieutenant-particulier* and *assesseu*r in Poitiers, various *conseillers magistrals* at the presidial seat of justice of Poitiers, the Conservator of Royal Privileges at the University of Poitiers, the criminal lieutenant and *lieutenant particulier* from Fontenay-le-Comte, various royal officials from Niort, the seneschals of Montmorillon and Civrey, various royal officials from Saint-Maixent (including Michel le Riche, whose memoirs are a useful source for the history of this period), and numerous advocates, proctors, and "practitioners" from the presidial seat of justice of Poitiers.

Then the remaining deputies from the third estate are listed. They included the following: eleven deputies from Poitiers, including the mayor and eight *échevins*; two delegates from the town of Châtellerault; proctors for the towns of Fontenay-le-Comte, Montmorillon, Saint-Maixent, Civray, Parthenay, Dorat and Saint-Savin; a proctor for twelve individual inhabitants of Saint-Savin; a proctor for the inhabitants of Basse Marche; a proctor for the town and community of Saint-Benoît-du-Sault and the parishes of this *baillage*; a proctor for the parish of Vouvenil-sur-Vienne; two proctors for the parish of Chaillac, and three proctors representing eight other rural parishes.

Some of the delegates entered protests concerning the summons. For example, the representatives of the clergy and third estate of the town of Dorat protested that they should not have been summoned, because Dorat was not part of Poitou. The commissioners duly registered these protests.

Finally the presiding officers read a list of those declared in default. They had been summoned but had neither appeared nor sent proctors. It included the town of Niort, numerous parishes, the monks, abbot, and monastery of La Celle in Poitiers, and various towns and *châtellenies,* such as the town of Mortemar and the *châtellenie* of Herbiers.

It is clear from the above that the representation had been greatly extended since the assembly of 1514. For the first estate it seems to have been increased to include royal and collegiate churches and parish priests, although it is to be noted that only six of the latter attended. Judging by the number of nobles present, it is probable that the summons had been extended to those with middle and low justice, although this cannot be proved. The representation of the third estate had been greatly extended. It appears that every town, village, parish, *châtellenie*, and lesser seat of justice in Poitou was invited to send delegates.[113]

It is evident that this extension of representation occurred some time between 1514 and 1559. Unfortunately, the information concerning the composition of the assemblies of the three estates of Poitou between the two dates is too limited to permit a definite conclusion as to precisely when this took place. It does not seem to have occurred before the reign of Henry II, and it is quite possible that the assembly of October 1559 was the first at which representation was extended to any considerable degree.

The next question to be examined is whether or not this increase in representation proved to be permanent. If so, it will be interesting to note its effect upon the composition of assemblies of the estates of Poitou during the period 1560 to 1651. Information concerning the delegates for the clergy is the most plentiful, and perhaps the most instructive.

We have seen that in 1559 the representation from the clergy was apparently extended to include royal and collegiate churches and parish priests. Although very few parish priests actually attended, the number of clergymen or their proctors present was much greater than it had been in 1514. In 1560 an entirely new procedure was adopted. Instead of being summoned directly to the assembly of the three estates of the province, the clergy were summoned to preliminary assemblies in each

---

[113] This assumption is based on the large number of towns, villages, *châtellenies*, parishes, and lesser seats of justice that were represented, and on the even larger number that were listed as being in default. This representational extension is in keeping with the findings of A. Babeau, "La représentation du Tiers Etat aux assemblées pour la rédaction des coutumes au XVIe siècle", *Revue Historique*, XXI (1885), 91-100. He concludes that, in the assemblies for the codification of the custom laws during the reign of Louis XII only church dignitaries and the principal benefice holders were summoned for the first estate and only towns were represented in the third estate. At the assemblies for the recodification of the custom during the reign of Henry II, however, he concluded that parish priests were generally summoned from the first estate, and rural parishes, villages, *baillages*, and lesser seats of justice were represented in the third estate.

of the three dioceses of Poitou. At each of these meetings a small number of delegates was chosen to represent the clergy of the diocese at the assembly of the estates of Poitou. As might be expected, this reduced the number of clergymen who actually attended the meeting of the three estates of the province. Such preliminary elections were held by the clergy prior to each assembly of the estates of Poitou during the period 1560-1651.

In spite of preliminary elections, the number of deputies who attended the assembly of the clergy of Poitou on October 28, 1560 was still quite large. All told, thirty-eight clergymen were present.[114] Although less than the number present in 1559, this was nearly twice as many as in 1514, when only about twenty had attended. The first deputy listed in the *procès-verbal* was the vicar general of the bishop of Poitiers. Next followed a representative of the bishop and clergy of Maillezais, and a representative of the bishop and clergy of Luçon, both of whom had been elected in preliminary assemblies of their respective dioceses. Next were listed fourteen deputies elected in a preliminary assembly of the diocese of Poitiers. They included representatives of the dean, canons, and chapter of the Cathedral of Poitiers, the dean, canons, and chapter of Saint-Hilaire-le-Grand, the canons and chapter of Sainte Radagonde, the canons and chapter of Notre-Dame-la-Grande, and the church of Saint-Pierre-le-Puellier. All of the above churches and chapters were in Poitiers. Also present were eleven representatives of twelve monasteries (of whom five were the abbots), one representative of two collegiate churches in Thouars, one representative of the collegiate church of Parthenay, two representatives of the archpriest, deans, canons, chapter and clergy of Notre-Dame de Châtellerault, one delegate from the clergy of the barony of Saint-Maixent, one representative of the clergy of the *châtellenie* of Montreuil-Bonnin, three priors or their representatives, and the curé of Notre-Dame-la-Grande of Poitiers. No priests from rural parishes were present. It should be noted that only sixteen of the thirty-eight deputies had been elected in preliminary diocesan assemblies. At all subsequent meetings, a much higher proportion was elected in these preliminary assemblies.

Only nineteen deputies attended the assembly of the clergy of Poitou on October 17, 1576.[115] All of them came from the diocese of Poitiers, with the exception of the vicar general of the bishop of Maillezais. The

---

[114]   *A. H. P.*, XX, 325-34. By this time the deputies from the three orders deliberated separately in Poitou.

[115]   A. D. Vienne, G 399, Oct. 1 and Oct. 17, 1576.

diocese of Luçon was not represented, as it sent its own deputy directly to the Estates General. Ten of the deputies had been elected in a preliminary assembly of the diocese of Poitiers. Eight of them came from the town of Poitiers. The other two chosen were the archdeacons of Briançay and Thouars. The vicar general of Maillezais was probably elected in a preliminary assembly of that diocese. Most of the eight remaining deputies were representatives of various monasteries throughout the diocese of Poitiers.

There are several interesting points to be noted about the composition of this assembly. In the first place, only half as many deputies were present as in 1560, and approximately the same number as in 1514. In the second place, in contrast to the situation in 1560, more than half of the deputies had been elected in preliminary diocesan assemblies. There may well have been a direct connection between this latter fact and the marked reduction in the number present. Finally the disproportionately large representation of the diocese of Poitiers, and particularly of the town of Poitiers, should be noted.

Very little information is available about the composition of the assemblies of the clergy of Poitou on August 25, 1588 and August 21, 1614. Amongst those present at the former assembly were four delegates of the chapter of Saint-Hilaire-le-Grand.[116] The deputies on August 21, 1614 included the bishop of Poitiers, the deans of the cathedrals of Poitiers and Luçon, and three delegates from the chapter of Saint-Hilaire.[117]

Only seven deputies from the first estate attended the meeting of February 26, 1649, and all of them seem to have been elected in preliminary diocesan assemblies.[118] Five of these delegates represented the diocese of Poitiers, and the other two represented the dioceses of Maillezais and Luçon.

Twelve delegates attended the assembly of the clergy of July 3, 1651, ten of whom came from the diocese of Poitiers.[119] All five of the men who had represented the diocese of Poitiers in 1649 were again present, and the same men represented the diocese of Luçon. Maillezais sent a different delegate, and five additional representatives were present from the diocese of Poitiers. They included three canons and a curé from Poitiers, and the prior of Charroux. Once again, the small

---

[116] Collection de Dom Fonteneau, LX, 457.
[117] *Ibid.* Also *Mémoires de René de Brilhac, A. H. P.*, XV, 10-49.
[118] A. D. Vienne, G 411, Feb. 23 and Feb. 26, 1649.
[119] *Ibid.*, July 3, 1651. Also Mss. de la Bibliothèque de Poitiers, 304 (42).

number present, the predominance of the clergy from the town of Poitiers, and the absence of any rural parish priests, are to be noted.

From the above, it is evident that the number of delegates for the clergy attending assemblies of the three estates of Poitou during the period 1560 to 1651 never approached the number that had attended the meeting of October 1559 for the recodification of the customs. Thirty-eight clergymen were present at the assembly of October 1560, but at subsequent meetings even fewer attended than in 1514. This is not surprising in view of the fact that preliminary assemblies were held in 1560 and thereafter. It would not necessarily indicate any real decrease in representation providing that all of the elements which had been represented in 1559 were represented at these preliminary assemblies. Whether or not this was the case is the next question to be examined.

The only diocesan assembly held to elect deputies for the meeting of the three estates of Poitou for which the list of those present is available is that of the diocese of Poitiers on October 1, 1576.[120] Only twenty clergymen were present, sixteen of whom came from the town of Poitiers. Those from the town included eight canons from the cathedral, the representatives of Saint-Hilaire, Sainte-Radagonde, Notre-Dame-la-Grande, and Saint-Pierre-le-Puellier. The four delegates from outside the town were the archdeacons of Briançay and Thouars, the dean of Champigny, and the archpriest of Faye. No country curés were present. These twenty clergymen elected half of their number to attend the meeting of the three estates of Poitou later that day. They reported back to the assembly of the diocese that afternoon. Those present again are listed, and include a few abbots, or their representatives, in addition to those who had attended in the morning.

Information is also available about the composition of several assemblies of the diocese of Poitiers held between the years 1611 and 1651 for purposes other than the election of deputies to meetings of the three estates of Poitou.[121] It cannot be proven that the composition of such assemblies would be the same as when deputies were being chosen to attend meetings of the estates of Poitou. It was similar enough, however, to the composition of the diocesan assembly of October 1, 1576 to lead one to suspect that this was the case. Royal letters of February 28, 1615 confirmed the right of the chapter of Saint-Hilaire to send two delegates to assemblies of the diocese. At a diocesan assembly a few years later, the abbot of Montierneuf was chosen to replace the abbot

---

[120]   A. D. Vienne, G 399, Oct. 1, 1576.
[121]   *Ibid.*, G 403 and G 1310. Also Collection de Dom Fonteneau, XII, 469.

of Charroux to represent all of the abbots of the diocese at future meetings. At a later assembly, it was stipulated that, in future, the following could attend; two delegates for the cathedral chapter of Poitiers, two representatives from the chapter of Saint-Hilaire, the abbot of Montier-neuf to represent all abbots, the priors of Sainte-Radagonde and Saint-Denis de Poitiers to represent the priors of the diocese, one delegate to represent the out-of-town chapters (*chapitres forains*), the archpriest of Lusignan and the dean of Châtellerault for the archpriests, rural deans and curés. At an assembly of the diocese on July 29, 1651, it was decreed that the canons of Sainte-Radegonde, Notre-Dame-la-Grande, and Saint-Pierre-le-Puellier, could, "as accustomed", each name a deputy to diocesan assemblies.

It is evident then that representation at assemblies of the diocese of Poitiers was quite restricted. During the seventeenth century, five men represented all of the abbots, priors, archpriests, rural deans, and curés of the diocese. At least in the case of the curés, one might suspect that this representation was more nominal than real.

Whether the representation was equally restricted in the other two less densely populated dioceses of Poitou is difficult to say. For Maillezais the only detailed information available concerns an assembly of May 4, 1573.[122] In this case, the vicar-general wrote to all the archpriests and deans of the diocese instructing them to summon all abbots, priors, curés, religious communities, and all other benefice holders. When the assembly was held, a number of parish priests actually attended. On April 24, 1610 the bishop of Luçon (the future cardinal Richelieu) summoned the abbots, deans, canons, curés, and other benefice holders to attend a synod of the clergy of that diocese.[123] Attendance at these assemblies in Luçon was apparently compulsory, as in 1609 Richelieu fined two abbots for failure to attend.[124] In June 1614 Richelieu received instructions from the governor of Poitou to summon "all the clergy of your diocese" to elect one deputy to attend a meeting of the estates of Poitou which was being held to choose deputies to the Estates General.[125] Exactly whom Richelieu actually summoned on this occasion cannot be determined. Apparently then, representation in both the dioceses of Maillezais and Luçon was less restricted than in the diocese

---

[122] *A. H. P.*, XX (1889), 352-61.
[123] B. N., ms. fr. 22,884, no. 56, published by Lacroix, *Richelieu à Luçon*, pp. 76-78.
[124] Lacroix, *Richelieu à Luçon*, p. 76.
[125] Archives des affaires étrangères, t. 769, fol. 169, published by Lacroix, *Richelieu à Luçon*, pp. 204-205.

of Poitiers. It should be remembered, however, that Maillezais and Luçon only sent one representative each to meetings of the three estates of Poitou, while all the rest came from the diocese of Poitiers. Hence, even if the clergy of Luçon and Maillezais enjoyed more liberal suffrage at their diocesan assemblies, in the long run their representation at the estates of Poitou was very limited, unless voting was by diocese rather than by head, which does not seem to have been the case.

It appears then, that the great extension of representation which occurred for the first estate in 1559 had little permanent effect in Poitou. At least in the diocese of Poitiers, which elected the overwhelming majority of deputies for meetings of the clergy of the entire province, the conservative forces triumphed and gained control of the preliminary elections. The bishops, abbots, and chapters which had dominated assemblies of the clergy prior to 1559, found themselves suddenly swamped in the meeting for the recodification of the customs in that year. The introduction of preliminary assemblies in 1560 gave them their opportunity and, in the diocese of Poitiers at least, they promptly gained firm control of the preliminary diocesan assembly. In 1560, quite a number of deputies attended the meeting of the three estates without having participated in these diocesan assemblies, but, in subsequent years, this does not seem to have been the case. After 1560, most of the delegates present had been elected in these preliminary assemblies, and a marked reduction in their number is to be noted. Not only did no parish priests participate in any further meetings of the estates of the province, but their representation in preliminary assemblies of the diocese of Poitiers was nominal.

Unfortunately, information concerning the deputies from the nobles who attended assemblies of the three estates of Poitou after 1559 is extremely limited, except for the meeting of July 3, 1651. For most other assemblies, virtually the only information concerns the participation of the mayor and *échevins* of Poitiers. They were *noblesse de cloche*, which meant that they were nobles as long as they held office. In many towns, the *noblesse de cloche* sat with the third estate, but in Poitiers they had managed to win the right to have at least some of their number attend assemblies of the nobles by 1576, and perhaps by 1560. In 1559 they sat with the third estate.

The mayor and five *échevins* chosen by the town council of Poitiers attended the assembly of the nobles of Poitou on October 1, 1576.[126] The meeting of August 25, 1588 was poorly attended. The deputies

[126]   Régistres de Poitiers, reg. 42, Sept. 30, 1576.

included a number of country nobles from the Gâtine district of Poitou, four *échevins* of Poitiers, and probably the mayor as well.[127] At this assembly a bitter dispute arose concerning the right of the mayor and *échevins* of Poitiers to meet with the nobles. The result was a royal decision that, in future, the mayor and two *échevins* could attend, but that the two *échevins* would only have one vote between them.[128] On August 21, 1614, two *échevins* from Poitiers attended the assembly of the nobles, in accordance with the royal ruling.[129] It is interesting to note that one of them, René Brochard, was chosen by the *third estate* as deputy to the Estates General. At the assembly of February 26, 1649, the nobles were poorly represented.[130] Once again the mayor of Poitiers and two *échevins* attended.[131]

The detailed *procès-verbal* of the assembly of the three estates of Poitou on July 3, 1651 has been preserved, and provides considerable information about the deputies present for the second estate.[132]

According to the presiding officer, about three hundred nobles attended. The *procès-verbal* only lists two hundred and fifty-four, but another source actually lists over three hundred.[133] In addition, hundreds of other nobles sent letters of procuration which, as it turned out, were not accepted on the grounds that they had not been properly certified. Among those present was the mayor of Poitiers, accompanied by fourteen *échevins*.[134] Evidently the rule restricting the number of *échevins* who could attend had been abandoned. This time the *procès-verbal* states clearly the qualifications required for attendance. All nobles eighteen years of age and over residing in Poitou had the right to attend. Apparently they did not even have to be holders of fiefs.

It is clear then that a great extension in representation had taken place for the nobles since 1514, when only counts, viscounts, barons, *châtellains*, and seigneurs with high justice had been summoned. Due to lack

---

[127] B. N., ms. fr. 20,157, fol. 153; also Ouvré, "Essai sur la Ligue à Poitiers", *M. S. A. O.*, ser. 1, XXI, 148-49; Régistres de Poitiers, reg. 48, Aug. 22, 1588.
[128] See below, pp. 126-27.
[129] *Mémoires de René de Brilhac, A. H. P.*, XV, 10-49; Régistres de Poitiers, reg. 69, Aug. 19, 1614.
[130] Debien, "La question des Etats-Généraux de 1649 et de 1651", *B. S. A. O.*, X, 609.
[131] Régistres de Poitiers, reg. 100, Feb. 22, 1649.
[132] Mss. de la Bibliothèque de Poitiers, 304 (42).
[133] Debien, "La question des Etats-Généraux de 1649 et de 1651", *B. S. A. O.*, X, 622-28. Debien publishes a list which appeared in installments in the *Affiches du Poitou* during the year 1780. The original existed at that time in the archives of the chateau of Touffou.
[134] Régistres de Poitiers, reg. 102, July 3, 1651.

of information, it is impossible to establish exactly when the extension took place, but the large number of nobles who attended the assembly of October 1559 suggests a widening of the summons by this date. As the second estate in Poitou did not normally hold preliminary elections, it became possible for large numbers of nobles to attend the meetings of the three estates of the province. Presumably from lack of interest, they did not always do so. We have seen that in 1588 and 1649 the nobles were poorly represented. However, at the assembly by July 3, 1651, over three hundred nobles attended, as compared with twelve deputies for the clergy and thirty-three for the third estate. Perhaps the greater interest shown by the nobles this time can be explained in part by the fact that the meeting was held during the *Fronde*, although this argument is weakened by the fact that the assembly of February 26, 1649 was poorly attended.

Just as for the nobles, information about deputies from the third estate concerns chiefly those from the town of Poitiers, except for the assembly of July 3, 1651. On October 28, 1560, the delegates for the third estate included deputies from the towns of Poitou and royal officials.[135] Four deputies chosen by the town council of Poitiers were present at the assembly of October 1, 1576.[136] At the meeting of August 25, 1588, the representation of the town of Poitiers seems to have been larger.[137] Each of the town's twenty-three parishes was invited to choose two delegates, who were to be notable persons and devout Catholics. In addition, the town council selected two deputies. On August 21, 1614, the delegates for the third estates included two royal officials, both of them counsellors at the presidial seat of Poitiers, two bourgeois chosen by the town council, and one representative of the community of merchants of Poitiers.[138] The town of Saint-Maixent had been invited to send one or two delegates but declined to do so, having no specific grievances.[139] The town of Niort was also invited to send delegates but the meeting at which they were to be elected was so poorly attended that the mayor called it off.[140] Presumably then, Niort sent no delegates,

---

[135]   *Journal de Jean de Brilhac, A. H. P.*, XV, 1-9.
[136]   Régistres de Poitiers, reg. 42, Sept. 30, 1576.
[137]   *Ibid.*, reg. 48, Aug. 18 and Aug. 22, 1588.
[138]   *Ibid.*, reg. 69, Aug. 18, 1614. Also, *Mémoires de René de Brilhac, A. H. P.*, XV, 10-49.
[139]   *Archives de Saint-Maixent*, B. B. 2, *Inventaire-Sommaire des archives communales antérieures à 1790 de Saint-Maixent*, ed. Richard. Also Richard, "Recherches sur l'organisation communale de Saint-Maixent", *M. S. A. O.*, Ser. 1, XXXIV, 360.
[140]   Favre, *Histoire de la ville de Niort*, pp. 233-34.

unless they were selected by the town council. The third estate seems to have been poorly represented at the assembly of February 26, 1649.[141] Several secondary *sénéchaussées* of Lower Poitou had not had the time or the desire to hold elections. The only two deputies for the third estate of the entire province whose names are known, are the delegates of the secondary *sénéchaussée* of Montmorillon.

All of the names of the deputies of the third estate who attended the assembly of the estates of Poitou on July 3, 1651, are known, as they are listed in the *procès-verbal*.[142] Thirty-three delegates of the third estate were present, thirty of whom came from the town of Poitiers. They included four representatives of the town council and twenty-six delegates from fourteen of the parishes of Poitiers. The other nine parishes in the town apparently did not name any representatives. The three deputies who did not come from Poitiers were representatives of secondary *baillages* of the province. They included the seneschal and the fiscal advocate from Thouars and a master apothecary representing the *baillage* of Parthenay.

The number of deputies from the third estate present in 1651 was considerably smaller, then, than the number present in 1559 and only slightly in excess of that of 1514. As in the case of the clergy, this is to be expected in view of the fact that preliminary elections were introduced in 1560. Unlike the clergy of the diocese of Poitiers, however, the third estate retained in its preliminary assemblies the wide representation which had been granted in 1559.[143] It appears that virtually every secondary seat of justice, village and country parish in Poitou continued to be represented in these preliminary assemblies, just as they had been at the meeting of October 1559 for the recodification of customs.

To sum up then, the representation at assemblies of the three estates of Poitou was quite restricted until the mid-sixteenth century. It was then greatly extended for all three orders as shown by the composition of the meeting for the recodification of customs in October 1559. This did not prove to be permanent for the first estate, as the conservative

---

[141] Debien, "La question des Etats Généraux de 1649 et de 1651", *B. S. A. O.*, X, 609. This can also be inferred, in spite of some tears in the document, from the *Journal de M. Demaillasson, A. H. P.*, XXXVI, 6 which states that "no deputies were present from other royal seats (sic) and towns other than those of (sic) ——— with those of the town of ———".

[142] Mss. de la Bibliothèque de Poitiers, 304 (42).

[143] For a description of these preliminary assemblies of the third estate, see above, pp. 91-93.

elements which had always dominated the assemblies of this order soon regained control, at least in the diocese of Poitiers. This extension of suffrage did continue for the other two estates, however, although in the case of the third estate, the number of deputies who actually attended the estates of Poitou was kept small by the introduction of preliminary assemblies. Finally it should be noted that the town of Poitiers dominated assemblies of the third estate in the same way that the diocese of Poitiers dominated meetings of the first estate.

Why this extension in representation took place is a question of some importance, and one which is rather difficult to answer. One recent historian of French representative institutions, J. R. Major, concluded that it was fairly general in many parts of France during the latter half of the sixteenth century, and suggests several possible reasons, two of which could be applicable to Poitou.[144]

The first possibility is that the suffrage was expanded on the orders of judges of the Parlement of Paris presiding over assemblies for the codification of customs. This can probably be rejected as a general answer to the problem throughout France as a whole because of the wide variety of procedure followed, even in areas where the same men presided. However it does appear that the well-known royal judge Christofle de Thou may have had some influence, for in the areas where he presided over assemblies for the recodification of customs between 1555 and 1582, a general extension of suffrage is discernible.[145] In Poitou, the influence of de Thou may well have been an important factor in explaining the extension of representation. It was he who presided over the assembly of October 1559, and it was at this meeting that this extension seems to have occurred for the first time.

The second possibility is that it took place on the orders of local royal officials. Indeed, in most cases, it seems to have been they who had the greatest influence upon the suffrage, as it was they who were normally charged with the convocation of the *baillage* estates. The royal letters usually instructed them to proceed "in the accustomed manner", the precise procedure to be followed being left in their hands. In cases where the actions of local royal officials did lead to an extension of the suffrage, they may have been influenced by the well-known principle of Roman law *quod omnes tangit, debet ab omnibus approbari* (that which concerns all should be approved by all). They may have

---

[144] Major, *The Deputies To The Estates General*, pp. 124-28.
[145] See Filhol, *Le Premier Président Cristofle de Thou* for a detailed study of this topic.

sincerely believed that even parish priests and peasants were concerned and should be consulted. This concept had not led to an extension of suffrage earlier, as the quality of the voters rather than the quantity had been stressed. Major thinks that a greater interest in Roman law in the sixteenth century led to a more literal interpretation of *quod omnes tangit*. The evidence in Poitou is insufficient to permit any definite conclusions on this subject, but the theory certainly appears worthy of consideration as a possible explanation.

E. PAYMENT OF DEPUTIES

The only information about the payment of deputies who attended meetings of the three estates of Poitou concerns the delegates from Poitiers prior to about 1470. The town always paid the expenses of its deputies. As a rule, the receiver of extraordinary revenues was instructed by the town council to make the necessary payments.[146] In November 1416 a sergeant accompanied the delegates from Poitiers to the assembly at Thouars to keep track of their expenses.[147] In June 1417 the town receiver accompanied them to a meeting at Saumur for the same purpose.[148] They apparently travelled in considerable comfort with the town paying all of their expenses. In December 1420, in addition to the regular expenses of the three deputies who attended a meeting of the three estates in Saint-Maixent, 40 *sous* were paid to a sergeant who served them as valet, and 40 *sous* to their cook who also accompanied them.[149] The expense account for the deputies from Poitiers for their trip to the assembly of November 1416 in Thouars included servants and horses.[150]

The total cost to the town obviously varied with the length of the trip, the number of deputies, and perhaps the importance of the individuals. The expenses of the two deputies to the assembly at Thouars in November 1416 amounted to 16 *livres*, 6 *sols tournois*.[151] The longer trip to Saumur of four delegates in June 1417 cost the town 74 *livres*, 11 *sols*, 4 *deniers*.[152] The expenses for the three deputies for the meeting in Saint-Maixent on December 20, 1420 totalled 19 *livres*, 10 *sols*, 4

146   A. C. Poitiers, J 546-547; Régistres de Poitiers, reg. 3, fols. 36 and 72.
147   A. C. Poitiers, J 546-547.
148   *Ibid.*, J 554.
149   Régistres de Poitiers, reg. 2, fol. 72.
150   A. C. Poitiers, J 546-547.
151   *Ibid.*
152   *Ibid.*, J 554.

deniers.[153] The three delegates from Poitiers to the assembly at Bressuire in September 1461 received 15 *livres* to cover their expenses.[154]
Usually then, it cost Poitiers about 15 to 20 *livres* to send its deputies to
assemblies in other parts of the province. When the meeting took place
in Poitiers, the deputies from the town do not seem to have been paid
at all.

Although no information is available, it may be assumed that the
other towns of the province also paid the expenses of their delegates to
meetings of the three estates of Poitou. One may perhaps speculate that
abbeys and chapters also paid the expenses of their representatives but
that nobles and prelates attended at heir own expense. There is no
evidence to prove this definitely, however.

The complete lack of any information regarding the payment of
deputies who attended meetings of the three estates of Poitou after about
1470 may be explained in part by the fact that nearly all of these assemblies were held in Poitiers. Hence the delegates from that town incurred virtually no expenses. The archives of other towns in the province are somewhat fragmentary and tell nothing about the payment of
their deputies. Most of the information about delegates for the clergy
concerns the diocese of Poitiers. Once again, the absence of references
to their payment can be explained by the obvious fact that their expenses
would be negligible when the three estates met in Poitiers.

F.   ORDERS MEETING TOGETHER OR SEPARATELY

The question of whether the three orders met together or separately at
assemblies of the estates of Poitou is of some interest. During the years
before 1470, it is not possible to tell with any certainty. Thomas believes
that the usual procedure in France during the fifteenth century was for
them to deliberate together.[155] Between 1470 and 1559 it can be stated
that the three estates of Poitou normally met together. Certainly they did
so on March 28, 1497, October 16, 1514, November 27, 1529, and
October 16-21, 1559.[156] Very little is known about the procedure followed in 1483. It appears, however, that the deputies elected by the
estates of Poitou to attend the Estates General were chosen by the three

---

[153]   Régistres de Poitiers, reg. 2, fol. 72.
[154]   A. C. Poitiers, J 1277.
[155]   Thomas, *Les Etats provinciaux*, pp. 54-55.
[156]   Rymer, V, part 2, 91; Bourdot de Richebourg, IV, 743-74; B. N., ms. fr.
20,084, p. 57; Bourdot de Richebourg, IV, 818-38.

orders together. Maurice Claveurier, a deputy from the third estate
stated later that he had been "commissioned and deputized by the
estates of the *pays* of Poitou".[157] Guillaume d'Appelvoisin, sire de Pigny,
a deputy from the second estate, declared that he had "attended the
Estates General for the estates of the *pays* of Poitou".[158]

In 1560, however, the procedure changed. At the meeting held on
October 28, of that year, and at all subsequent assemblies of the estates
of Poitou, the three orders met together at a brief opening session but
then separated to elect their deputies to the Estates General and to
prepare their *cahier* of grievances.

The reason why the three estates began to deliberate separately in
1560 is not entirely clear.[159] This policy was adopted later in the same
year by the Estates General. Clearly then, the estates of Poitou was not
imitating the national body. It does not seem to have been due to any
attempts to divide and rule. Certainly, no royal instructions, secret or
otherwise, indicate such a policy. In some parts of France the answer may
lie in the extension of suffrage. The nobles and clergy may have feared
that they would be swamped and outvoted by the delegates from the
villages and country parishes. This was not the case in Poitou, however, because the introduction of preliminary assemblies for the third
estate made this impossible. Neither does the answer lie in any fundamental antagonism between the three orders. Except for a slight anti-
clerical attitude shown by the lay estates, particularly in 1561, there is
nothing to indicate any special hostility between them. In 1560, the
year in which the orders separated for the first time, the *cahier* of the
clergy of Poitou actually contained a clause calling for the conservation
of the privileges of the nobles so that they should be in a position to
support the other estates and defend the Catholic religion.[160]

Just as was the case in explaining the extension of suffrage, the new
policy of the three estates meeting separately must be traced in large
part to the actions of local royal officials. Their motives are not entirely
clear. In Poitou they cannot have been motivated by a desire to avoid
the confusion of overly large meetings following the extension of the
suffrage as this was prevented by the introduction of preliminary assemblies in the first and third estates. It may be that the local royal
officials instructed the orders to meet separately so that they themselves

[157] B. N., p.o. vol. 772, doss. 17,625: Claveurier, no. 15.
[158] A. N., KK 648, fol. 92, no. 85.
[159] For a good general discussion of this problem, see Major, *The Deputies To
The Estates General*, pp. 129-30.
[160] *A. H. P.*, XX, 350.

could capture control of the third estate. They had little hope of controlling all three orders meeting together.

It is possible that the new policy was based entirely on convenience. Beginning in 1560, much of the time of the assemblies was devoted to the preparation of *cahiers* of grievances to be presented at the Estates General. Although there was no profound antagonism between the orders, it is evident from their lists of grievances that their interests were frequently different. A matter which might be of vital concern to the delegates of the third estate and to which they might devote much discussion and a large part of their *cahier*, might be of little or no interest to the clergy. Therefore, both the local royal officials and the deputies may have felt that the preparation of *cahiers,* and the election of the deputies who would present them, would be simpler and quicker if the three orders met separately.

G. PROCEDURE AT THE MEETINGS

Unfortunately, we have practically no information about the procedure followed at meetings of the three estates of Poitou prior to about 1470. No minutes of the meetings (*procès-verbaux*) have survived. In fact, very few *procès-verbaux* for any meetings of provincial estates in fifteenth century France have been preserved. Thomas was able to discover one for the estates of Haut-Limousin [161] and it is probable that the procedure was similar in Poitou. In addition we do have the brief report of Denis Dausseure, the single representative for all three estates of Poitou at the joint assembly of the estates of Poitou, Touraine, Anjou, Maine, Saintonge, and Angoumois held at Tours on January 10, 1464.[162] Although this was not a typical meeting of the estates of Poitou, it may give some clues as to the procedure generally followed at such assemblies. Judging from this latter account, and from the findings of Thomas, it seems that, when the estates had been summoned by the king, one of the royal commissioners opened the session by explaining to the assembly the purpose of the meeting.[163] If it was a case of voting a tax, he would explain the necessity for it and then request the specific amount called

[161] Published, Thomas, *Les Etats provinciaux*, Pièces Justificatives, no. 1.
[162] Régistres de Poitiers, reg. 4, fol. 123.
[163] For example, on January 10, 1464, Jean Dauvet and the other royal commissioners who presided over the joint assembly at Tours, began by describing the great expenses borne by the king for the conquest of Roussillon and for the repurchase of the towns of Picardy from the duke of Burgundy. They then asked the deputies to vote a *taille* of 100,000 *écus*.

for in the royal instructions. The deputies would then deliberate on the matter, tax or otherwise, and reach their decision. If they had been called to give advice, they would then present their recommendations. If they had been assembled to vote a tax, they would vote a precise amount. Sometimes they granted the amount requested by the king but, on some occasions, they voted less. When voting a tax, they might also make various requests to be presented to the king. The commissioners would then thank them for having granted the tax or for having given their advice, and dismiss them with the promise that any requests they had presented would be brought to the king's attention.

Before Poitou became part of the royal domain in 1422, the commissioners of John, duke of Berry, or of the dauphin Charles as count of Poitou, probably proceeded in a similar manner. In all probability, the procedure was also similar when the estates were convoked by the town council of Poitiers and the presiding officer whom the council had selected, replaced the commissioners.

Slightly more information is available about the procedure followed at meetings of the three estates of Poitou during the period 1470 to 1559. The only detailed *procès-verbal* that has survived was for the assembly of October 16-21, 1559,[164] but brief descriptions are also available of the meetings of March 28, 1497,[165] and October 16, 1514.[166]

The presiding officer opened the assembly of March 28, 1497 by reading the royal letters patent authorizing the meeting to take place. He then read the articles of the Treaty of Etaples which the estates had been summoned to ratify. Then he and the deputies confirmed and approved these articles and swore an oath to keep and observe them. The account of the proceedings was signed by the clerk (*greffier ordinaire*) of the *sénéchaussée*. It was then sealed with the seals of the *sénéchaussée* and of the lieutenant of the seneschal.

No information is available about the procedure at the meeting of the estates of Poitou of November 27, 1529 for the ratification of the Treaties of Madrid and Cambrai. However, brief descriptions of the assemblies of the estates of a number of other *baillages* and *sénéchaussées*, held during the same month and for the same purpose, have survived.[167] The fact that these descriptions were almost identical, leads one to

---

[164] Bourdot de Richebourg, IV, 775-839.
[165] Rymer, V, part 2, 91.
[166] Bourdot de Richebourg, IV, 743-74.
[167] Montferrand, B. N., ms. fr. 3086, fols. 98-109; Berry, *Ibid.*, fols. 110-121; Montargis, *Ibid.*, n.a., 1118, fols. 135-137; Orléans, *Ibid.*, fols. 138-142, and ms. fr. 6199, no. 3.

suspect that the procedure in Poitou was very similar. It seems to have been approximately the same as that followed at the meeting of March 28, 1497.

The detailed *procès-verbal* for the assembly of the three estates of Poitou of October 16, to October 21, 1559, gives a clear picture of the procedure followed at meetings for the codification of customs.[168] On October 16, the three royal commissioners, Christofle de Thou, president in the Parlement of Paris, and Barthélemy Faye and Jacques Violle, royal counsellors in Parlement, went to the assembly hall and the meeting began. The clerk read aloud the royal letters commissioning the above three men. Then Maître Jean Barbier, royal advocate at the presidial seat of justice of Poitiers, announced that the three estates of the *pays* and county of Poitou were summoned to appear before the royal commissioners on October 15, and the days following. The *procès-verbal* then lists those present. Presumably, they either presented their credentials or answered a roll call. The commissioners then called upon the deputies to swear the prescribed oath, the wording of which was stated in detail. They swore to report, loyally and conscientiously, what they had seen and observed of the ancient customs of Poitou. They promised also to give their opinions about them, stating in what ways they found them harsh or unreasonable, so that the commissioners might change and correct them as ordered in the royal instructions. Then, at 2:00 P.M. ,on Monday, October 16, the commissioners began to read aloud the printed list of customs as codified in 1514. They continued to do so all week, morning and afternoon, until Saturday noon. The different articles were discussed and some were altered on the advice of the deputies. Most of the changes consisted merely of adding or removing a few words for greater clarity. In some cases, an entire article was dropped or an entirely new one added. Thus, article by article, the new codification was completed. The *procès-verbal* states in each case to what article in the old codification the new article corresponded. On Saturday morning, October 21, the commissioners declared this new codification of the custom laws to be the law of Poitou. All three of them signed it and the assembly was dismissed.

The earlier codification of the custom laws of Poitou, made in October 1514, has survived along with a list of those present at the assembly.[169] No detailed *procès-verbal* of the meeting is included, but only a very brief description. As nearly as one can tell from this short ac-

[168] Bourdot de Richebourg, IV, 775-839.
[169] *Ibid.*, 743-74.

count, the procedure was very similar to that described above for the later meeting of October 1559.

As we have seen already, when the three estates of Poitou were summoned to elect deputies to the Estates General during the period 1560 to 1651, they met together for a brief opening session and then deliberated separately. No detailed information is available about the opening meeting in the years 1560, 1561, 1576 and 1588. The procedure followed in 1614, 1649 and 1651 can be described in some detail, however.[170]

The presiding officers were colorfully attired in red robes. On high seats to their right sat the deputies of the clergy. On high seats to the left of the presiding officers sat the deputies of the nobles with the mayor of Poitiers, as first baron of Poitou, occupying the first place. The delegates from the third estate sat together on lower seats. First were various royal officials. Next to them, in 1651 at least, sat the delegates from the town council of Poitiers. Next were the representatives of the various parishes of Poitiers and finally the delegates from the secondary *baillages* and *sénéchaussées*.

In 1651 at least, the assembly was open to the public. The chief presiding officer ordered the main door of the hall to be opened and a large crowd of people of all conditions entered. When the *huissiers* had imposed silence, he ordered the *lettres de cachet* calling for the convocation of the estates to be read and the meeting began.

On all three occasions, one of the presiding officers delivered an opening address explaining the purpose of the assembly. In 1651, he specified the voting requirements for nobles and the procedure to be followed by representatives of the second estate bearing letters of procuration. In 1614, after the opening address, the roll was called. This was probably done in other years as well. In 1651 those who had been summoned and had not attended were declared in default and were forbidden to hold any other assembly. Next, the presiding officers instructed the three orders to meet separately to elect their deputies and prepare their *cahiers*. As a rule, they specified the various halls in which these separate meetings would take place. The clergy and nobles then withdrew to the appointed locations while the deputies from the third estate remained where they were.

The procedure followed at the assemblies of the clergy can be de-

[170] The following are the sources of this information: 1614 – *Mémoires de René de Brilhac, A. H. P.*, XV, 10-49; 1649 – Régistres de Poitiers, reg. 100, March 1, 1649; 1651 – *Ibid.*, reg. 102, July 3, 1651, and Mss. de la Bibliothèque de Poitiers, 304 (42).

scribed in the most detail as the *procès-verbaux* from most of these meetings have survived.[171] In 1649 and probably at all of the assemblies, the procurations of the deputies were read first.[172] The presiding officer then called upon the assembly to proceed with the election of the number of deputies which had been stipulated in the royal instructions. Exactly how the voting was conducted cannot be determined. It is quite likely that a plurality of votes was considered sufficient. In 1560 and 1651 the three deputies chosen were declared to be elected unanimously.[173] In 1614 the election of Armand-Jean du Plessis de Richelieu, bishop of Luçon, seems to have been virtually arranged in advance, chiefly through the influence of the bishop of Poitiers.[174] Several letters from the latter to Richelieu during July and August show that he was doing everything possible to secure his election. On August 9 he informed Richelieu that he would be the only delegate from the clergy. On August 19 the bishop of Poitiers wrote to say that his election was assured but that it had been necessary to add the dean of St. Hilaire as a second delegate. Various reasons were given for this, the chief of which was to placate the clergy of the diocese of Poitiers. However, the bishop described the dean of St. Hilaire as "as peaceful a man as one could desire".

After the deputies had been elected to the Estates General, the delegates turned their attention to the preparation of the *cahier*. As a rule, they entrusted this task to a committee. In October 1576 they appointed ten of their number to receive the "memoirs, complaints, and grievances from the abbots, monasteries, monks, chapters, priors, curés, chaplains and others".[175] From these they would draw up the *cahier,* sign it, and turn it over to the delegates elected to present it at the meeting of the Estates General. In February 1649 they chose a committee of four to draw up the *cahier*, including two representatives of the diocese of Poitiers, and one from each of the dioceses of Luçon and Maillezais.[176] In July 1651 only one man was selected to prepare the *cahier.*[177] Perhaps only minor changes were to be made in that of 1649, making the task much simpler than usual.

[171]   *A. H. P.*, XX, 325-34; A. D. Vienne, G 399, Oct. 1, and October 17, 1576; *Ibid.*, G 411, Feb. 26, 1649; *Ibid.*, July 3, 1651.
[172]   A. D. Vienne, G 411, Feb. 26, 1649.
[173]   *A. H. P.*, XX, 325-34; mss. de la Bibliothèque de Poitiers, 304 (42).
[174]   Hanotaux, "La Jeunesse de Richelieu", *Revue des Deux Mondes*, XCIV, 599-600; Hanotaux, *Histoire du Cardinal de Richelieu*, I, 149-50.
[175]   A. D. Vienne, G 399, Oct. 1, 1576.
[176]   *Ibid.*, G 411, Feb. 26, 1649.
[177]   *Ibid.*, July 3, 1651.

The procedure followed on October 28, 1560, was slightly different.[178] The presiding officer offered the delegates the alternatives of either presenting the grievances of their various churches, chapters, etc., to be approved by the assembly, or of choosing a committee to work on the *cahier*. The procedure chosen was, in a sense, a combination of these two alternatives. First of all, a canon of Saint-Hilaire-le-Grand of Poitiers, presented a list of grievances of the chapters, monasteries and abbeys of the town of Poitiers. This list was read to the assembly and approved. Then the representative of the clergy of Luçon presented the list of grievances of his diocese which was read and approved. The representative of the clergy of Maillezais did the same. A committee of seven, including one of the deputies elected to attend the Estates General, was then chosen to prepare the final draft of the *cahier*. As it was getting late, the assembly adjourned for the day. The delegates were instructed to think about the *cahier* over night and submit any suggestions in the morning to the presiding officer or to any member of the committee. At eight o'clock the next morning, the committee met in the house of the presiding officer and drafted the final form of the *cahier*. It was signed by the presiding officer, by all seven members of the committee, and by the notary who had written the *procès-verbal*.

Sometimes a number of assemblies were required before the *cahier* could be completed. In 1576 the clergy met on October 1, 2, 3, and 17 for this purpose.[179] In 1614 the clergy held a preliminary assembly on August 12, presumably to commence the compilation of their *cahier*. The three orders met together on August 21 and on August 24 each chose its deputies. The following week or so was devoted by the clergy to the completion of its lists of grievances. Richelieu went in person to Poitiers to take part in the discussion and the completed *cahier* contains many of his personal views. It was not until September 4 that the final copy of the *cahier* of the clergy of Poitou was given to Richelieu and the dean of Saint-Hilaire.[180]

Unfortunately, the only two assemblies of the nobles about which much information is available, are those of August 25, 1588 and July 3, 1651. Both sessions were stormy and gave rise to a number of procedural disputes which will be discussed later. In 1614 and 1651 the

---

[178] *A. H. P.*, XX, 325-34.
[179] A. D. Vienne, G 399, Oct. 1, and Oct. 17, 1576.
[180] Hanotaux, "La Jeunesse de Richelieu", *Revue des Deux Mondes*, XCIV, 600-601; Hanotaux, *Histoire du Cardinal de Richelieu*, I, 150; Lacroix, "Richelieu à Luçon", *M. S. A. O.*, XII, 283.

nobles elected a committee to draft their *cahier*.[181] It is probable that this was the usual procedure. In 1651 they entrusted the task of preparing the *cahier* to two men who had recently been made nobles, Jean Gabriau de Riparfond and Charles Boynet de la Touche-Fressinet.

The only description of the meetings of the third estate which has survived, concerns that of July 3, 1651.[182] The vote was collected by the presiding officer, Martin Reveau, particular lieutenant and civil assessor in Poitiers. Reveau had presided over the joint meeting of the three estates and had remained in the assembly hall to supervise the assembly of the third estate when the other two orders withdrew. The third estate elected two deputies by a plurality of votes. They then chose "unanimously" a committee of four to draw up their *cahier*. Those selected for this purpose were a royal *élu*, a lawyer, a royal proctor, and a merchant, all from Poitiers. As the third estate also chose a committee to prepare their *cahier* in 1614,[183] one may perhaps conclude that this was their usual practice.

Frequent procedural disputes occurred during the election of deputies to the Estates General in Poitou, especially at the assemblies of the nobles. For example, a bitter dispute took place at the meeting of the nobles on August 25, 1588 over the right of the *échevins* of Poitiers to attend this assembly and cast their votes.[184] At least two issues were involved. In the first place, most of the country nobles were supporters of the League while the *échevins* were loyal to the king. Hence, the former were seeking to prevent the *échevins* from voting by contesting their right to do so. In the second place, the traditional scorn of the nobles of the sword for the *noblesse de cloche* was undoubtedly involved. Many of the country nobles withdrew, held a separate assembly, and elected Pierre de la Chapellerie, seigneur de Rouilly, as their delegate. The *échevins* of Poitiers and a few other nobles then held another assembly and elected the count of Sanzay, colonel-general of the *arrière-bans* of France and hereditary *parageur* of Poitou. The seigneur de Rouilly, in the meantime, had gone to Blois and had his candidature confirmed by the Estates General. Sanzay then arrived to take his seat. The case was brought before the king who confirmed the candidature of both men. The question of the right of the *échevins* of Poitiers to

---

[181] *Mémoires de René de Brilhac, A. H. P.*, XV, 10-49; Mss. de la Bibliothèque de Poitiers, 304 (42).

[182] Régistres de Poitiers, reg. 102, July 3, 1651; Mss. de la Bibliothèque de Poitiers, 304 (42).

[183] *Mémoires de René de Brilhac, A. H. P.*, XV, 10-49.

[184] Ouvré, "Essai sur la Ligue à Poitiers", *M. S. A. O.*, XXI, 148-49.

attend assemblies of the nobles of Poitou was then debated by the delegates of the second estate present at the meeting of the Estates General. They decided that henceforth the mayor of Poitiers and two *échevins* chosen by the town council could attend assemblies of the nobles.[185] The two *échevins* would only have one vote between them, however, and would sit after all other nobles. This decision was confirmed by Henry III in March 1589.[186] It was adhered to in 1614 and 1649, but not in 1651.

Three extremely interesting disputes occurred at the assembly of nobles of July 3, 1651. The first was over who should preside and collect the votes.[187] The mayor of Poitiers claimed this right as first baron of Poitou and an argument ensued. To settle the matter, the nobles finally sent for Martin Reveau, particular lieutenant and civil assessor of Poitiers who had presided over the joint opening assembly of the three estates. Reveau collected the votes in spite of the protests of the mayor.

The second dispute concerned the election of the royal lieutenant of Poitou, the marquis of la Rocheposay, as deputy for the nobles.[188] When Reveau arrived at the assembly of the nobles at about 5 P.M., he was presented with a signed statement of opposition to the election of this man on the grounds that he was a royal lieutenant. It was alleged that at an assembly of the nobles of France which had been held in Paris, it had been decreed that no one holding such an office should be chosen as a deputy for this meeting of the Estates General. This assembly in Paris, moreover, had been approved by the king. There was also a further reason for objecting to the election of la Rocheposay. As royal lieutenant, it was he who had received the royal letters of convocation in Poitou. Those opposed to his election claimed that he had not passed them on to Reveau until two months after their date and that, during this two month period, he had made arrangements to secure his own election. They requested that his election be declared null and void, and that a new vote be taken. Reveau admitted that he had not received the royal letters of convocation until two months after their date and that this had prevented him from holding the assembly earlier. He declared that the election of the marquis of la Rocheposay would be decided by

---

[185] *Ibid.* Also Régistres de Poitiers, reg. 48, Aug. 29, 1588; Collection Dom Fonteneau, XXIII, 185. A. C. Poitiers, M, Reg. 15, fol. 68.
[186] *Ibid.*
[187] Régistres de Poitiers, reg. 102, July 3, 1651.
[188] Mss. de la Bibliothèque de Poitiers, 304 (42).

the royal Privy Council. In the meantime, he instructed the nobles to vote again and elect two deputies with la Rocheposay eligible. Some nobles threatened to walk out and hold a separate election but Reveau forbade them to do so. A new vote was held and this time the marquis of la Rocheposay and the count of Bessay were elected. Reveau was about to leave the assembly about 8 P.M. when he was met by a group of nobles who had opposed the candidature of la Rocheposay and had withdrawn, but now demanded the right to vote. In spite of some opposition, Reveau agreed to accept their votes. The election was not yet settled for a third dispute then arose.

This time, the dispute concerned vote by proxy. Usually in France, votes by proxy were accepted without question when there were no rival candidates.[189] When the election was hotly contested, however, the presiding officer sometimes refused to count them. In 1651 vote by proxy had been specifically authorized in the royal letters of convocation.[190] At the opening session of the three estates of Poitou, Reveau had announced that all nobles bearing letters of procuration were to swear with their hands between his, that all the persons named in their letters were nobles, residing in Poitou, and eighteen years of age or over. These procurations were then to be certified by a *procureur royal* of the seat of justice of Poitiers and there would be severe penalties for fraud. As Reveau was about to leave the assembly of nobles at about 9 P.M., the *procureur royal* in charge of certifying the letters of procuration arrived on the scene, declared that he had not yet been able to complete the task, and requested more time. Also, some more nobles arrived who had not yet voted. It was by then too dark to see and Reveau adjourned the meeting until seven o'clock the next morning.

When they assembled again the next morning, la Rocheposay and Bessay claimed that Reveau should not count the votes of those nobles who had arrived late the previous day and had not yet voted. The latter group protested that he had promised to do so. Reveau decided that he would accept the votes of all present who had not voted yesterday but that he would then sign and close the *cahier* and not accept any votes by proxy, so that any further argument might be avoided. He then counted the votes of those who had not yet voted and declared that they were all for la Rocheposay and Bessay. He then signed and closed the *cahier*.

His troubles were not yet over, however. The *procureur royal* who had been examining the letters of procuration then stated that he had

---

189   Major, *The Deputies To The Estates General*, pp. 119-20.
190   *Ibid.*, p. 122. Also Mayer, VII, 386-87.

checked them all. There were two hundred and twenty-six letters representing the votes of three hundred and thirty-four nobles and they were all for the marquis of Oirvau as deputy. The noble who had presented these letters of procuration then swore to Reveau that they all represented nobles residing in Poitou, eighteen years of age or over. The *procureur royal* declared that he believed them to be genuine, but was not prepared to accept the responsibility and the punishments prescribed by a new law if they were not. Then Reveau was presented with a veritable flood of letters of procuration. One *procureur royal* gave him three letters representing the votes of fifteen nobles, all cast for the marquis of Oirvau. He also was willing to certify them by an oath of credulity only. Another noble had three hundred and fifty letters representing four hundred nobles, all voting for the marquis of Oirvau. Two other nobles presented seven letters and twelve letters respectively, all representing votes for Oirvau. They all demanded that Reveau accept these votes by proxy. Some of them claimed that they had been unable to find a *procureur royal* willing to certify these letters of procuration because they all feared the new penalties for fraud. Then another *procureur royal* declared that he had been given between six hundred and seven hundred letters of procuration, all of them representing votes for la Rocheposay and Bessay. Reveau stuck to his original decision and refused to accept any votes by proxy on the grounds that none of them had been properly certified by *procureurs royaux*. He gave a signed act of protest to all those who objected, which they could use, if they so desired, to bring their case before the regular legal courts or the royal council. He then recounted the votes cast in person on both days and announced that la Rocheposay and Bessay had many more votes than any other candidate. He declared the marquis of la Rocheposay to have been legally elected as first deputy for the nobles of Poitou and the count of Bessay to be second deputy. He forbade the nobles to hold any more assemblies about this matter and told them that they could present their protests to the royal council. He then officially closed the assembly.

There are a number of possible reasons for Reveau's refusal to accept votes by proxy. It is possible that he sincerely doubted the authenticity of many of the letters of procuration and felt that they had not been properly certified. He may have been trying to simplify a very complicated situation and seized upon a technicality to justify his action. There is a third possibility that cannot be excluded, however. It is possible that he was anxious to see a royal official elected, such as the marquis of la Rocheposay, who might be expected to be loyal to Mazarin and the king. When he saw that many of the votes by proxy were for a rather turbulent noble, the marquis of Oirvau, he may have decided to exclude them. If so, the technical point that many *procureurs royaux* feared to certify the letters of procuration except by oath of credulity (if at all), provided him with his opportunity.

The assemblies of the clergy for the election of deputies to the Estates General were more orderly, but even there a few minor procedural disputes occurred. For example, at the meeting of February 26, 1649, an objection was made to the letter of procuration of the subprior of the Cathedral of Maillezais.[191] He claimed to represent not only the clergy of the diocese of Maillezais, but also the bishop of La Rochelle. The difficulty was due to the recent transfer of the bishop of Maillezais to La Rochelle. The assembly decided to accept him only as the representative of the clergy of Maillezais.

Another minor procedural dispute occurred at the same meeting. The royal letters of convocation called for each estate to name only one deputy. Some delegates remonstrated that it was customary for the clergy of Poitou to choose two delegates, one from the higher clergy and one from the lower. It was pointed out, however, that it was also customary for the other orders to select two deputies each. Hence, seeing that the other orders were in the same position, the clergy decided to adhere to royal instructions and elect only one deputy.

No record has survived of any procedural disputes at assemblies of the third estate of Poitou. It is quite likely that some occurred, however.

When the *cahier* of each order had been completed, it was presented to the royal official who had presided over the joint opening session of the three estates. He signed them all and gave them to the deputies who had been elected to present them at the Estates General.[192] The only official *procès-verbal* which has survived, that of 1651, was signed by the chief presiding officer, by a *procureur royal,* and by a clerk. This normally completed the procedure for the election of deputies. One exceptional case should be noted briefly, however. The royal letters of convocation in 1561 called for an unusual procedure.[193] The estates of each *baillage* and *sénéchaussée* were to elect three deputies, one from each estate, to attend an assembly in the principal town of each *gouverne-*

---

[191] A. D. Vienne, G 411, Feb. 26, 1649.

[192] *Mémoires de René de Brilhac, A. H. P.,* XV, 10-49; Mss. de la Bibliothèque de Poitiers, 304 (42).

[193] See J. R. Major, "The Third Estate In The Estates General of Pontoise, 1561", *Speculum* (April, 1954), XXIX, 465.

ment where, in turn, one deputy was to be elected from each order to attend the meeting of the Estates General. The probable purpose of this procedure was to save the people money and to avoid the confusion of too large an assembly. Poitou at this time formed part of the *gouvernement* of Guyenne. Because of the size of this *gouvernement*, its governor, Anthony of Bourbon, King of Navarre, issued orders on the last day of February 1561, that two different assemblies would be held, one at Bordeaux and one at Angoulême.[194] We know that deputies from Poitou attended the meeting at Angoulême on March 20, 1561, along with deputies from Saintonge, the town and *gouvernement* of La Rochelle, and Aunis.[195] Presumably, the estates of Poitou had met some time before this date to elect deputies to attend this assembly. The *gouvernement* of Guyenne did not comply precisely with the royal instructions to send only one deputy from each estate. Instead, the third estate was unable to come to any agreement and sent one deputy from each *sénéchaussée*.[196] This was the only time the *gouvernements* elected deputies to the Estates General.

[194]   B. N., Collection des Cinq Cents de Colbert, XXVII, fol. 303.
[195]   *Ibid.*, fol. 325. Probably deputies from Angoumois also attended this meeting.
[196]   Major, "The Third Estate In The Estates General Of Pontoise", *Speculum*, XXIX, 466.

CONCLUSIONS

Prior to about 1470 the role of the three estates of Poitou consisted largely of consenting to taxes and giving advice to their feudal lord on matters of local interest. After about1470 they met only for four specific purposes: to ratify treaties, to codify the customs of the province, to protest to the king about salt taxes, and to elect deputies and prepare lists of grievances for meetings of the Estates General. Therefore, it must be admitted that the scope of their activities was somewhat restricted and that their role in French history was modest.

Nevertheless, the estates of Poitou served a useful purpose. During the first half of the fifteenth century, it was a valuable medium through which John, duke of Berry and Charles VII could obtain the consent of the influential inhabitants of the province to the taxes which they needed so desperately to carry on the war with the English. It also provided a useful means for the king to keep in touch with the most powerful churchmen and nobles and the most important towns, in order to keep them informed of his plans and needs and, on occasion, to receive their advice. Such regular contact between the king and his subjects was one of the chief characteristics of the Renaissance monarchy in France which owed much of its strength to its popularity. In later years, when the king sought to have a treaty ratified by the chief individuals and corporative groups of the kingdom or to have the customs of the various provinces codified, local estates, such as those of Poitou, provided him with the means. After 1483 they also provided the local framework for the elections of deputies and the preparation of lists of grievances for meetings of the Estates General. When the people of Poitou and the adjoining provinces had a serious grievance, as in the mid-sixteenth century over the salt taxes, the local estates served as a useful medium through which they could present their requests to the king.

At all times throughout its existence then, the estates of Poitou kept alive some contact between the king and the people of that province. When it ceased to meet after 1651, this was one sign that the popular monarchy of the Renaissance had been replaced by the absolute monarchy of Louis XIV.[1] One of the chief causes for the fall of the French monarchy in the eighteenth century was the fact that the king had lost touch with his people. When Louis XIV ceased to summon the estates of many of the provinces of France, including Poitou, it was clearly a step in this direction.

Finally, let us attempt to fit the estates of Poitou into the broader picture of French provincial estates in general. Prior to about 1435, there seems to have been no fundamental difference in nature between the estates of Poitou and those of Brittany or Languedoc. After this date, however, the three estates of Poitou no longer met to vote royal taxes, while those of some provinces, such as Brittany and Languedoc, continued to do so. During the latter years of the reign of Charles VII, the distinction between *pays d'état* and *pays d'élection* became valid for the first time. Poitou fell into the latter category along with most of the provinces of central France. Henceforth, the estates of Poitou resembled those of Limousin, La Marche, and Périgord, meeting only occasionally for a few purposes.

The estates of the *pays d'élection* have been sadly neglected by historians, partly because their histories are not spectacular and partly because their sources are usually fragmentary. In fact, for many years, the work of Thomas provided almost the only detailed study in this field to which other historians could refer. While his work is sound, it is restricted to a small area and a short period of time. Before a definitive history of French provincial estates can be written, much research remains to be done on the estates of other *pays d'élection*, such as Anjou, Touraine, Orléanais, Berry, Saintonge, and Angoumois. If this history of the estates of Poitou has done something to fill this gap, it has served its purpose.

---

[1] The estates of Auvergne, Rouergue, Quercy, Périgord, Saintonge, La Marche, Bourbonnais, Berry, Touraine, Orléanais, Picardy, and Normandy also met for the last time between 1651 and 1662. Like the reign of Charles VII, then, the early years of the reign of Louis XIV must be regarded as a critical period in the history of French provincial estates.

APPENDIX A

CATALOGUE OF ASSEMBLIES [1]

1. *December 1, 1372, Loudun* – Various clergymen, nobles, and townsmen of Poitou assembled and signed a treaty with French military commanders regarding the return of Poitou to French control.[2]

   *1375, between March 26 and June 14 – Possible assembly to grant John, duke of Berry, a tax of twelve *deniers* per *livre* on all merchandise sold in Poitou for three years.[3]

   *1381, April or May, Niort – Possible joint assembly of the estates of Poitou and Saintonge to advise John, duke of Berry, about conditions in the region, which was partly in the hands of the English and which was being pillaged by armed bands.[4]

2. *c. 1382* – Voted *fouage* of fifteen *francs* per parish to John, duke of Berry. Seem to have imposed certain conditions regarding its collection.[5]

3. *November, 1390* – Granted a tax of 10,000 *livres* to the count of Montpensier, son of John, duke of Berry.[6]

4. *November, 1391* – Granted 10,000 *francs* to the count of Montpensier to help him to "maintain his estate".[7]

[1] * Indicates a possible meeting. ** Indicates one order meeting alone. Only definite meetings of the three estates are numbered.

[2] Delachenal, IV, 432-36; Froissart, *Chroniques*, VIII, pp. CLV-CLIX; B. N., ms. fr. 3,910, fol. 111; Guérin, *A. H. P.*, XIX, 176-90, 199-205, and 367-72.

[3] *Régistre de Barthélemi de Noces*, pub. Teilhard, *Bib. Ec. Ch.*, LII, 230, 517, and 554.

[4] D'Aussy, "La Saintonge pendant la Guerre de Cent Ans", *Bulletin de la Société des A. H. S. A.*, XIV, 221. Also *Régistres de L'Echevinage de Saint-Jean d'Angély (1332-1496)*, pub. d'Aussy, *A. H. S. A.*, XXIV, 258-59.

[5] A. N., X1c 46 B, no. 207.

[6] Fillon, ed., *Documents pour servir à l'histoire du Bas Poitou*, I.

[7] B. N., ms. fr. 6,742.

5. *1393, prior to September 20* – Voted 40,000 *écus* to John, duke of Berry.[8]

6. *1395* – Voted 40,000 *francs* to John, duke of Berry.[9]

7. *February, 1396* – Granted 40,000 *francs* to John, duke of Berry, to help him meet the expenses of the "mariage d'Armeignac".[10]

8. *1399* – Granted 40,000 *écus* to John, duke of Berry.[11]

   **1402 (prior to April 27), Saint Maixent – Assembly of the clergy of Poitou. Granted an *aide* to the king to be used for the war. It was to be paid "in the customary sum and manner" by the clergy of Poitou for a three year period beginning October 1, 1401, just as the prelates of the kingdom assembled at Paris had agreed to do for the same three year period.[12]

   *August, 1404 – Possible joint meeting with the estates of Périgord, Limousin, Angoumois, and Saintonge to grant a *fouage* for the siege of Courbefy by the constable, Charles d'Albret.[13]

9. *March, 1406* – Estates of Poitou, Limousin, Périgord, Angoumois, and Saintonge, meeting separately, voted a *fouage* to de Torsay, de Harpedenne, and other French commanders to be used in a campaign to retake Brantôme, Carlux, and Limeuil, which had recently revolted.[14]

8   A. C. Poitiers, H 10.
9   La Trémoïlle, ed., *Livre de comptes de Guy de la Trémoïlle et Marie de Sully, 1395-1406*, pp. 21-22.
10 *Computi Particulares In Rotulo Dyny Rapponde Tangentes Dominum de Tremoillya*, ed. La Trémoïlle, *Les La Trémoïlle pendant cinq siècles*, I, 1-10. The "Armagnac marriage" referred to was undoubtedly that between the duke of Berry's eldest daughter Bonne and Bernard d'Armagnac in 1393. The money was presumably for a dowry.
11 A. N., KK 254, fol. 35 v°.
12 B. N., ms. fr. 20,886, fols. 108, 109, and 110.
13 Jules Machet de la Martinière, "Les guerres anglaises dans l'ouest et le centre de la France, 1403-1417" (Unpublished thesis for the Ecole des Chartes, 1899), Position de thèse, p. 2, hereafter cited as La Martinière, "Les guerres anglaises". Only a brief synopsis of these theses for the Ecole des Chartes, known as a *position de thèse*, is made available to the public, and it does not, as a rule, contain footnotes. Hence, it is not possible to check La Martinière's sources. It is likely that he discovered some documents which have escaped the present writer, possibly in some town archives in one of the regions concerned other than Poitou. Probably all three of the assemblies that he mentioned, in 1404, 1406, and 1409, took place.
14 *Ibid.* This time, La Martinière's source is cited in the *Position de thèse* as Archives de la Dordogne, fonds Audierne, series E, ville de Périgueux, March 14, 1406. The pertinent passage, written in the dialect of Périgord, is quoted and there

*1409 (latter part) – Possible assembly of the estates of Poitou, Périgord, Saintonge, and Angoumois to vote a *fouage* for a campaign of constable d'Albret in Périgord.[15]

10. *July 1411, Niort* – Voted an *aide* of 41,000 *écus* to John, duke of Berry.[16]

11. *September 29, 1412, Poitiers* – Voted an *aide* of 10,000 *écus* to John, duke of Berry, to meet the threat of an English invasion of the province.[17]

12. *November 1412, Poitiers* – Assembled to advise the duke of Berry regarding the English invasion.[18]

13. *December 22, 1412, Bressuire* – Assembled again to advise the duke of Berry regarding negotiations for the withdrawal of the English from Poitou.[19]

14. *February 1413, Bressuire* – Purpose and results unknown.[20]

15. *May 2, 1413, Saint-Loup* – Summoned by John, duke of Berry. Purpose and results unknown.[21]

16. *May 1415, Niort* – Granted 50,000 *livres* to the duke of Berry.[22]

May 1416, Niort – Possible joint meeting with the estates of Saintonge. Purpose unknown.[23]

---

is no doubt about this series of assemblies. See also Cardenal, "Catalogue des assemblées des Etats de Périgord", p. 250, which describes the assembly of the estates of Périgord on March 14, 1406 to vote this *fouage*.

[15] La Martinière, "Les guerres anglaises", Position de thèse, p. 8. The fact that a *fouage* was imposed in Périgord by constable d'Albret in the latter part of 1409 is shown by G. Charrier, ed., *Les Jurades de la ville de Bergerac* (Bergerac, 1892), I, Jurades of October 20, November 8, November 14, December 1, 1409, and January 8, 1410.

[16] A. C. Poitiers, K 4.

[17] Lacour, "Une incursion anglaise", *A. H. P.*, XLVIII, 1-87. This appears to be the earliest document referring specifically to the "gens des Troys Estaz" of Poitou. It goes on to explain that this means the "clergy, nobles, and inhabitants of the good towns of our said *pays* of Poitou".

[18] *Ibid.*

[19] *Ibid.* Also Régistres de Poitiers, reg. 1, fols. 19 and 20, and Ledain, "Maires de Poitiers", p. 329.

[20] B. N., ms. fr. 6,747, fol. 20 r°.

[21] Régistres de Poitiers, reg. 1, fols. 26, 27, 28, 30, and 31. Also Ledain "Maires de Poitiers", p. 329.

[22] Régistres de Poitiers, reg. 1, fols. 75, 76, and 78. Also Ledain, "Maires de Poitiers", p. 331.

[23] La Martinière, "Les guerres anglaises", Position de thèse, p. 13. Circumstantial

17. *November 17-22, 1416, Thouars* – To discuss with commissioners sent by the dauphin Charles, negotiations which he was conducting with Jean l'Archevêque, seigneur of Parthenay. The latter, an adherent of the duke of Burgundy, had been carrying on a bloody struggle in Poitou with the followers of the powerful Richemont.[24]

18. *June 1417, Saumur* – Pledged obedience to the dauphin Charles as new count of Poitou. Also protested against the pillaging of bands of Bretons and Picards who were followers of Richemont and the seigneur of Parthenay respectively.[25]

19. *1418 (Spring)* – Joint meeting with the estates of Saintonge, Limousin, Périgord, Angoumois, and La Marche, probably at Limoges. Granted the king 100,000 *francs* of which Poitou's share was 40,000 *livres*. Also requested that two royal commissioners be sent to Poitiers for some unspecified reason.[26]

20. *October, 1418* – Voted 42,000 *livres* to the dauphin. Assembly probably held at Niort.[27]

21. *Ca. December 1420* – Granted 42,000 *francs* to the dauphin.[28]

22. *November 25, 1421, Poitiers* – Joint assembly with the estates of Saintonge, Angoumois, and Limousin, presided over by Bernard d'Armagnac, lieutenant-general for the dauphin between the Loire and the Dordogne. Purpose unknown.[29]

---

evidence supporting La Martinière's statement is provided by D. d'Aussy, ed., *Archives de la ville de Saint-Jean d'Angély, Régistres de l'échevinage de Saint-Jean d'Angély, A. H. S. A.*, XXXII, 167, hereafter cited as *Régistres de Saint-Jean d'Angély, A. H. S. A.*, which state that on May 26, 1416, the town council of Saint-Jean d'Angély heard a report of one of its members who had been to Niort to appear before the Grand Master of Crossbowmen (Jean de Torsay) concerning the welfare of the province.

[24] A. C. Poitiers, J 546 and 547.
[25] *Ibid.*, J 553 and 554. Also Bélisaire Ledain, *Histoire de la ville de Parthenay, de ses anciens seigneurs, et de la Gâtine du Poitou* (Paris, 1858), p. 211.
[26] A. Thomas, "Nouveaux documents", *Annales du Midi*, XXV, 341. Also B. N., ms. fr. 22,731, fol. 23.
[27] Régistres de Poitiers, reg. 1, fols. 129-132; Also B. N., ms. fr. 22,731, fol. 23.
[28] A. C. Poitiers, J 644. Also Beaucourt, I, 405.
[29] Thomas, "Nouveau Documents", *Annales du Midi*, XXV, 441. Thomas cites as his source *Régistres de Saint-Jean d'Angély*, CCXIX, A. H. S. A., XXXII, 330. This document refers only to the towns and barons of Saintonge, Limousin, and Angoumois meeting in Poitiers on November 25. Although the estates of Poitou is not mentioned, it is reasonable to assume, as does Thomas, that it also participated since the assembly was held in Poitiers.

23. *July 1422, Poitiers* – Granted 20,000 *écus* to the king (presumably the regent) "for the conduct of the war, as well as for the making of good money".[30]

24. *November or December 1423, Saint-Maixent* – Voted a direct tax of 30,000 *livres tournois* per year for three years in lieu of the indirect taxes which had been granted by the Estates General at Selles in August 1423.[31]

25. *November 1, 1424, Poitiers* – Voted 50,000 *livres tournois* as Poitou's share of a tax of one million *livres* which had been granted to the king by the Estates General meeting in Poitiers during the previous month.[32]

26. *October or November 1425* – Voted an additional sum (*frais*) to be imposed over and above Poitou's share of a general tax which had been granted to the king by the Estates General meeting in Poitiers in November of that year. This additional sum was to be used for the payment of various royal officials.[33]

27. *December 1425, Saint-Maixent* – Joint meeting with the estates of Saintonge to deliberate regarding measures to stop the pillaging of lawless bands of soldiers. Summoned by the constable Arthur de Richemont.[34]

---

[30] B. N., ms. fr., n.a. 5233, no. 10.

[31] B. N., p.o., vol. 47, Amboise, no. 59; vol. 89, Argenton; vol. 247, Beaumont, doss. 5423, no. 2; vol. 1612, Labbé, doss. 37,421, no. 3; vol. 2855, Torsay, doss. 63,456, no. 11; vol. 201, La Barre, no. 9; *A. H. P.*, XX, 307-08; H. Imbert, *Histoire de Thouars* (Niort, 1871), p. 153. M. Vallet de Viriville, "Mémoire sur les institutions de Charles VII", *Bibliothèque de l'Ecole des Chartes*, XXXIII, 28, refers to this meeting, but dates it incorrectly as December 16, 1422. Imbert, p. 153, dates it as December 16, 1423. Régistres de Poitiers, reg. 2, fol. 51, November 30, 1423, states that the mayor and five bourgeois will be paid for a four day trip to Saint-Maixent on November 25 in compliance with royal orders. This would suggest that the assembly was held on this latter date rather than on December 16.

[32] Lacour, "Documents sur les Etats Généraux", *A. H. P.*, XLVIII, 91-117; B. N., p.o., vol. 247, Beaumont, doss. 5423, no. 3; vol. 1612, Labbé, doss. 37,421, no. 4; vol. 2855, Torsay, doss. 63,456, no. 13; vol. 772, Claveurier, doss. 17,625, no. 2; vol. 365, Blandin, doss. 7912, nos. 3, 4, 5, 6, and 7.

[33] Lacour, "Documents sur les Etats Généraux", *A. H. P.*, XLVIII, 112-13.

[34] Ledain, "Maires de Poitiers", pp. 348-49, describes this assembly, although he was not aware that it was held jointly with the estates of Saintonge. However, the source which he cites is incorrect. Ledain was usually a reliable historian, but this particular work was published posthumously, so that he had no chance to correct any errors. As a result, there are a few mistakes in his footnotes. In this case, part of his account is substantiated by Régistres de Poitiers, reg. 2, fol. 72,

28. *May 1, 1426, Saumu*r – Joint assembly with the estates of Anjou, Maine, Saintonge, Limousin, and Touraine. Summoned by the constable de Richemont. Purpose unknown.[35]

   **March 20, 1428, Niort* – Assembly of the barons of Poitou to discuss means of putting an end to the constant pillaging of lawless bands of soldiers.[36]

29. *1429 (after July), Poitiers* – Granted the king 60,000 *livres tournois* to help pay for the expenses of his coronation which had just been held at Rheims. The town of Poitiers later obtained a reduction of 12,600 *livres* in the tax.[37]

30. *September 1430, Chinon* – Granted the king 40,000 *livres tournois*. Also voted an additional 4500 *livres* to cover grants to various royal officials.[38]

31. *March 1431, Poitiers* – Summoned by the king. Complained bitterly about the violence of the lawless bands of soldiers.[39]

32. *1433, Niort* – Joint assembly with the estates of Saintonge. Voted a *fouage* to the king. Also voted 4000 *livres tournois* to Jean de la Roche (Rochefoucault), seneschal of Poitou, to besiege the town of Aubeterre which was held by the English.[40]

33. *August, 1434, Tours* – Joint assembly of the estates of Poitou, Saintonge, Anjou, and Touraine. Voted a tax to the king of which Poitou's share was 30,000 *livres tournois* plus various additional amounts for *frais*, which brought the total up to 43,656 *livres*, 10

Jan. 4, 1426. The fact that the assembly was held jointly with the estates of Saintonge is indicated by d'Aussy, "La Saintonge pendant la Guerre de Cent Ans", *Bulletin de la Société des A. H. S. A.*, XIV, 382. D'Aussy's source is also incorrect. However, his statement is substantiated by *Régistres de Saint-Jean d'Angély*, BB 28 and CC 8, *A. H. S. A.*, XXXII, 378. It was probably from these sources that d'Aussy drew his information.

[35] This information appeared in the report of a secret messenger from Tours who was unable to find out the purpose or the results of the meeting. Beaucourt, II, 588-89; E. Cosneau, *Le Connétable de Richemont* (Paris, 1886), p. 122.

[36] Régistres de Poitiers, reg. 2, fol. 90; Ledain, "Maires de Poitiers", p. 355.

[37] A. C. Poitiers, H 25, J 905 and J 906. In order to obtain this reduction, it was necessary to bribe several members of the king's council.

[38] B. N., ms. fr. 20,594, no. 25; *Ibid.*, p.o., vol. 2896, Le Tur, doss. 64,363, no. 11; *Ibid.*, vol. 1849, Mareuil, doss. 42,690, nos. 24 and 31; A. Thomas, "Les Etats Généraux sous Charles VII", *Revue Historique*, XL (1889), 70.

[39] Ledain, "Maires de Poitiers", p. 362. Ledain's source for this information is not indicated.

[40] B. N., Collection Clairambault, 194, fol. 7691.

sols tournois. The estates of Poitou also took up once again the matter of the 4000 *livres* promised to Jean de la Roche in the previous year for the siege of Aubeterre. As he had not yet received any of it, they agreed that he should be paid 1000 *livres tournois* from the *taille* which they had just voted, plus a further 2000 *livres* to be imposed over and above the principal of the tax. They also promised de la Roche another 4000 livres if he would stop pillaging the province and if he would use his men to drive out various other lawless bands.[41]

34. *1435 (prior to June 15), Poitiers* – Voted an annual direct tax of 61,500 *livres tournois* for four years in lieu of the *aides* which had been reestablished for a four year period by the Estates General of western Languedoil meeting in Poitiers in January of that year. Also voted an additional sum of 1125 *livres tournois* for payments to various royal officials.[42]

35. *1436 (between February and April)* – Voted a tax of 2300 *livres tournois* to be imposed on Poitou over and above their portion of the *taille* which had been granted to the king by the Estates General of Languedoil in February of that year. This money was to pay for a wedding gift from the province to the dauphin.[43]

36. *August 1440, Niort* – Assembly to discuss means of putting a stop to the pillaging of various partisans of the Praguerie, notably Jean de la Roche and the duke to Alençon.[44]

37. *March 1445* – Purpose and location unknown.[45]

38. *January 1446, Thouars* – Purpose unknown. The account of the receiver for Languedoil and Languedoc for the year ending Sep-

[41] Several documents refer to this assembly, usually calling it the meeting of the three estates in Tours, without being more specific. Beaucourt, II, 631, cites it as an assembly of the Estates General of Languedoil, but Thomas, "Les Etats Généraux sous Charles VII", *Revue Historique*, XL, 55-88, makes no mention of it. The true nature of this meeting is shown by B. N., p.o., vol. 3041, Vousy, doss. 67,419, no. 3. Further information is provided by A. N., K 63, no. 36; B. N., ms. fr. 20,886, fol. 114; La Boutetière, "Rôle des tailles en Poitou", *M. S. A. O.*, II, 499; and B. N., Collection Clairambault, 194, fol. 7691.

[42] B. N., ms. fr. 25,969, no. 956; *Ibid.*, ms. fr. 20,594, no. 27; *Ibid.*, p.o., vol. 2404, du Puy du Fou, doss. 53,880, no. 14.

[43] *Ibid.*, vol. 1324, Gilier, doss. 29,964, no. 22; A. N., K 64, no. 11.

[44] Régistres de Poitiers, reg. 3, fol. 36; Ledain, "Maires de Poitiers", p. 377.

[45] The only reference to this meeting is in the Régistres de Poitiers, reg. 3, fol. 70, March 9, 1445, which states, "Des plus notables de la maison de ceans seront vendredi aux trois estaz."

tember 30, 1446 shows that the estates of Poitou voted an additional sum over and above their share of a *taille* imposed by the king on Languedoil in January of that year to cover payments to various dignitaries. Possibly they made this grant at the assembly in Thouars.[46]

39. *November 10, 1446, Poitiers* – Summoned by the town of Poitiers to add their protests to a petition being prepared by the town council to send to the king in an attempt to dissuade him from establishing the *gabelle* in Poitou.[47]

40. *Late 1446 or 1447 (prior to March 31)* – Voted the king 18,000 *livres tournois* to be freed from the investigation of a royal commissioner whom he had sent to Poitou to investigate crimes and misdemeanors committed by various officials in the fields of justice and finance.[48]

41. *January 1447* – Voted various additional sums to be levied over and above Poitou's share of a *taille* of 200,000 *livres tournois* which the king had just imposed on Languedoil. These additional sums were to cover grants to a number of dignitaries.[49]

42. *November 1447, Poitiers* – Prepared a petition complaining of ills of all kinds which the province suffered from brigandage, stressing the resultant poverty and begging for a reduction in the *taille*. Chose a delegation to take this petition to the king.[50]

43. *Year ending September 30, 1448* – The account of the receiver-general of all finances in Languedoil and Languedoc for this year shows grants of small sums of money by the estates of Poitou to two royal officials. There is nothing to indicate when or where these grants were made.[51]

44. *Ca. December 1450* – Decided to send a delegation to the king to try and dissuade him from imposing the *gabelle* in Poitou.[52]

---

[46] *Ibid.*, fol. 72; B. N., ms. fr. 32,511, fols. 100-102; Gustave Dupont-Ferrier, *Gallia Regia* (Paris, 1942-54), IV, 469.

[47] Régistres de Poitiers, reg. 3, fol. 81.

[48] La Boutetière, "Rôle des tailles en Poitou", *M. S. A. O.*, II, 502; B. N., ms. fr. 20,887, fol. 1; *A. H. P.*, XXIX, 413-18; *Ibid.*, XXXI, 117-81.

[49] B. N., p.o., vol. 3041, Vousy, doss. 67,419, no. 6; *Ibid.*, ms. fr. 32,511, fols. 113 ro and 115 ro; *Ibid.*, 6200, p. 229; A. N., KK 648, fol. 91, no. 84.

[50] Régistres de Poitiers, reg. 3, fol. 89; B. N., ms. fr. 20,084, p. 43.

[51] *Ibid.*, ms. fr. 32,511, fol. 124 ro and vo.

[52] Régistres de Poitiers, reg. 4, fol. 19; A. C. Poitiers, J 1117 and J 1118. Also *Mémoires présentés au roi Charles VII*, *A. H. P.*, II, 253-84.

45. *Ca. 1451-1454* – Shortly after the French conquest of Guyenne, the estates of Poitou, Saintonge, and Angoumois met to make arrangements for workers to bring back into cultivation lands ruined by the war.[53]

46. *May 6, 1454, Poitiers* – Decided to send a request to the king asking that the indirect *aides* which he had established in 1451 be replaced in Poitou by an equivalent *taille*. As it was rumoured that the king was coming soon to the province, the delegates dispersed and went home. They were to be notified as soon as he left Tours for Poitiers.[54]

47. *July 18, 1454, Poitiers* – As the rumours of the royal visit proved to be unfounded, the three estates of Poitou met again regarding the same matter. They sent a delegate to the king to see if he would receive their deputation and, if so, where. His reply was favorable and a delegation was sent to the king on September 11.[55]

48. *August 9, 1461, Poitiers* – Met to discuss sending a delegation to Louis XI to seek abolition of the *aides*.[56]

49. *September 1461, Bressuire* – Convoked to deliberate on the same subject by the seigneur de Belleville who had been sent to Poitou as a royal commissioner to receive oaths of loyalty to the new monarch. Decided to send a delegation to the king instructed to do everything possible to secure the abolition of the *aides*.[57]

50. *January 10, 1464, Tours* – Joint assembly of the estates of Poitou, Touraine, Anjou, Maine, Saintonge, and Angoumois. Consented to a *taille* of 100,000 *écus* to help meet the cost of Louis XI's conquest of Roussillon and repurchase of the towns of Picardy from the duke of Burgundy. Complained, however, about the heaviness of taxes in general and requested that they be diminished.[58]

[53] A. N., X²ª41, plaidoiries du 4 mars, 1477. The document does not indicate whether this assembly took place after the French conquest of Guyenne in 1451 or after the reconquest in 1453.
[54] Régistres de Poitiers, reg. 4, fol. 41; A. C. Poitiers, M, reg. 11, fol. 34 v⁰.
[55] A. C. Poitiers, J 1206, J 1207 and J 1211. Also Mss. de la Bibliothèque de Poitiers, 385 (36), pp. 584-86.
[56] Régistres de Poitiers, reg. 4, fol. 91, Aug. 8, 1461.
[57] *Ibid.*, September 25, 1461. Also A. C. Poitiers, J 1277 and J 1279.
[58] Régistres de Poitiers, reg. 4, fol. 123, Jan. 17, 1464; B. N., ms. fr. 20,084, p. 46; Viollet, III, 238. This assembly is referred to also in Archives Communales d'Amboise, AA 144, but Abbé C. Chevalier, *Inventaire analytique des archives communales d'Amboise* (Tours, 1874), pp. 356-57, dates it incorrectly as Janu-

51. *August 20, 1466, Poitiers* – The king had written to the clergy and bourgeois of Poitiers inviting them to send their written observations on abuses in the administration of justice and finance and on the pillaging of soldiers to royal commissioners in Etampes. The clergy and bourgeois of Poitiers assembled and decided to summon the three orders of the province to add their opinions. Accordingly, on August 20, the three estates of Poitou met, drew up a list of grievances and suggestions and chose two delegates to take this list to the royal commissioners.[59]

52. *Year ending September 30, 1467* – Account of the receiver general for Languedoil shows that the estates of Poitou granted 600 *livres tournois* to Louis de Crussol, seneschal of Poitou.[60]

53. *Year ending September 30, 1468* – Account of the receiver general for Languedoil shows that the estates of Poitou granted a further 600 *livres tournois* to Louis de Crussol, seneschal of Poitou.[61]

54. *Year ending September 30, 1470* – Account of the receiver general for Languedoil once again shows 600 *livres tournois* granted by the estates of Poitou to Louis de Crussol.[62]

55. *Ca. December 1482, Poitiers* – To ratify the Treaty of Arras between France and Burgundy.[63]

56. *Ca. December 1483* – To elect deputies and prepare lists of grievances for the Estates General which met in Tours in January 1484.[64]

57. *March 28, 1497, Poitiers* – To ratify the Treaty of Etaples with England.[65]

58. *October 16, 1514, Poitiers* – To codify the customs of Poitou.[66]

59. *November 27, 1529, Lusignan* – To ratify the Treaties of Madrid and Cambrai.[67]

---

ary 10, 1483.

[59] Régistres de Poitiers, reg. 6, August 2, and August 27, 1466.

[60] B. N., ms. fr. 32,511, fol. 277 vo.

[61] *Ibid.*, fol. 283 ro.

[62] *Ibid.*, fol. 318 ro.

[63] A. C. Poitiers, M, reg. 11, fol. 1 ro.

[64] B. N., p.o., vol. 772, doss. 17,625, Claveurier, no. 15; A. N., KK 648, fol. 92, no. 85. This latter document is poorly copied and incorrectly transcribed in B. N., ms. fr. 6200, p. 299, vo.

[65] Rymer, V, part 2, 91; A. N., P 2302, pp. 789-92.

[66] Bourdot de Richebourg, IV, 743-74; A. C. Poitiers, M, reg. 11, fol. 59 vo.

[67] Bouchet, p. 453; B. N., ms. fr. 20,084, p. 57; *Ordonnances des rois de France,*

**Ca. December 1529 or January 1530* – Assembly of the nobles of Poitou. Voted one tenth of the revenue from their *fiefs* and *arrière-fiefs* for one year to pay their share of the ransom of Francis I and his sons.[68]

**April 28, 1549, Tarbes* – Possible joint assembly of deputies from Poitou and all other provinces and *sénéchaussées* under the jurisdiction of the lieutenant-governor of Guyenne. Its purpose is uncertain, but it may have been concerned with complaints against the *gabelle*.[69]

60. *July 11, 1549, Poitiers* – Joint assembly of the estates of Poitou, Châtellerault, Saintonge, the town and *gouvernement* of La Rochelle, Angoumois, Haut and Bas Limousin, Haute and Basse Marche, and Périgord. Offered the king 450,000 *livres* if he would abolish the *gabelle* and restore the *quart* and *demi-quart*. Chose six delegates to go to the royal court to complete the arrangements.[70]

61. *November 1549, Poitiers* – Joint assembly of the estates of Poitou, Châtellerault, Saintonge, the town and *gouvernement* of La Rochelle, Angoumois, Haut and Bas Limousin, Haute and Basse Marche, and Périgord. Apportioned among themselves the 450,000 *livres* which had been granted to the king to replace the *gabelle* by the *quart et demi-quart*, plus an additional 25,000 *livres* to reimburse the receivers of the salt warehouses who had purchased their offices.[71]

62. *November 18, 1549, Poitiers* – Estates of Poitou met alone regarding the apportionment of the above tax. It ordered that within a week it must receive a statement of the names and revenues of all nobles exempt from the *taille* so that their share of the tax could be fixed.[72]

---

règne de Francois, Ier, Académie des sciences morales et politiques, VI, part 1, 72-73.

[68] B. N., ms. fr. 15,637, fols. 154-56, 189-92, and 209-13; *Ibid.*, ms. fr. 5,497, fol. 265 vᵒ; Bouchet, p. 453; Ravan, "Etat des nobles du Poitou", *Mem. Soc. Statistique Deux-Sèvres*, ser. 2, I, 59-81.

[69] *A. H. P.*, IV, 314-15.

[70] Régistres de Poitiers, reg. 30, July 6, and July 10, 1549; *Documents inédits pour l'histoire du Poitou*, pp. 157-58; Bouchet, p. 574; B. N., Collection de Périgord, XXIV, fol. 343; Déruelle, "La révolte de la gabelle", pp. 192-93.

[71] B. N., Collection de Périgord, XXIV, fol. 336; Cardenal, "Catalogue des assemblées des Etats de Périgord", p. 255; Jurade de Bergerac du 7 novembre, 1549; Bouchet, p. 577; Thibaudeau, *Histoire du Poitou*, II, 231.

[72] Régistres de Poitiers, reg. 31, November 5, 1549; A. C. Poitiers, C 30.

63. *November 1549, Poitiers* – Joint assembly of the estates of Poitou, Saintonge, the town and *gouvernement* of La Rochelle, Angoumois, Haut Limousin, and Haute and Basse Marche. Selected their legal representatives to defend their interests in a dispute with the deputies of Bas Limousin and Périgord over the way in which the *quart et demi-quart* was to be enforced in these two provinces.[73]

   *1550, Poitiers – Assembly at which deputies from Poitou and Guyenne were present, probably concerning the above legal dispute. Possibly other provinces were also represented.[74]

64. *September 25, 1553, Poitiers* – Estates of Poitou met to discuss the cash offer to be made to the king for the repeal of the *quart et demi-quart*. Also chose deputies to attend a general assembly of the estates of all of the provinces concerned on October 1.[75]

65. *October 1, 1553, Poitiers* – Estates of Poitou, Saintonge, the town and *gouvernement* of La Rochelle, Angoumois, Haut and Bas Limousin, Haute and Basse Marche, Périgord, and Guyenne met and offered the king 1,194,000 *livres* to abolish the *quart et demi-quart*.[76]

66. *October 16-21, 1559, Poitiers* – To recodify the custom laws of Poitou.[77]

67. *October 28, 1560, Poitiers* – To elect deputies and prepare lists of grievances for the Estates General which met at Orleans in December 1560.[78]

68. *February or March, 1561*– Met sometime between February 14 and March 20 to elect deputies to attend an assembly at Angoulême on the latter date of delegates from the northern half of the *gouvernement* of Guyenne. At the assembly at Angoulême, deputies would be chosen to attend the Estates General which met at Pontoise in August 1561.[79]

---

[73] *Ibid.*, C 31.
[74] *Archives historiques du département de la Gironde*, XXVIII (1893), 49.
[75] Collection Dom Fonteneau, XXVII, ter., 141; A. C. Poitiers, C 33; Régistres de Poitiers, reg. 32, September 4, September 11, September 18, and September 21, 1553.
[76] *Ibid.*, Sep. 4, Sep. 18, and Sep. 21, 1553; A. C. Poitiers, C 33.
[77] Bourdot de Richebourg, IV, 775-839.
[78] A. D. Vienne, G 395, October 28, and 29, 1560; *Journal de Jean de Brilhac, A. H. P.*, XV, 1-9; *Lettres du Comte du Lude et autres personnages, A. H. P.*, XXVII, 35.
[79] B. N., Collection des Cinq Cents de Colbert, XXVII, fol. 303.

69. *October 1, 5 and 17, 1576, Poitiers* – To elect deputies and prepare lists of grievances for the Estates General which met at Blois in December 1576.[80]

70. *August 25, 1588, Poitiers* – To elect deputies and prepare lists of grievances for the Estates General which met at Blois in October 1588.[81]

71. *August 21, 1614, Poitiers* – To elect deputies and prepare lists of grievances for the Estates General which met in Paris in October 1614.[82]

72. *February 26, 1649, Poitiers* – To elect deputies and prepare lists of grievances for the Estates General which was scheduled to meet at Orleans in March 1649.[83]

73. *July 3, 1651, Poitiers* – To elect deputies and prepare lists of grievances for the Estates General which was scheduled to meet at Tours in September 1651.[84]

**June 1652 – Assembly of the nobles of Poitou, without royal consent, to discuss the disorders caused by lawless soldiers, and to petition the king to summon the Estates General as promised. Elected various officers, discussed meeting with the nobles of other provinces and decided to assemble again on July 1. The king issued orders forbidding this latter assembly.[85]

---

[80] Régistres de Poitiers, reg. 42, Sep. 17, Sep. 24, Sep. 27, and Sep. 30, 1576; A. D. Vienne, G 399, Oct. 1, and Oct. 17, 1576; *Journal de Guillaume et Michel le Riche*, Oct. 6, 1576; *Lettres addressées à Jean et Guy de Daillon, A. H. P.*, XIV, 78.

[81] Régistres de Poitiers, reg. 48, Aug. 22, and Aug. 29, 1588; Collection Dom Fonteneau, LX, 457; Ouvré, "Essai sur la Ligue à Poitiers", *M. S. A. O.*, ser. 1, XXI, 148-49; B. N., ms. fr. 20,157, fol. 153.

[82] *Mémoires de René de Brilhac, A. H. P.*, XV, 10-49; Hanotaux, "La Jeunesse de Richelieu", *Revue des Deux Mondes*, XCIV, 600-601; Hanotaux, *Histoire du Cardinal de Richelieu*, I, 150; Lacroix, "Richelieu à Luçon", *M. S. A. O.*, XII, 283.

[83] Merle, "Un cahier de doléances", *Bul. Soc. Hist. Sc. Deux-Sèvres*, IX, 90-91; *Journal de M. Demaillasson, A. H. P.*, XXXVI, 6; Régistres de Poitiers, reg. 100, Feb. 8, Feb. 22, and Mar. 1, 1649; A. D. Vienne, G 411, Feb. 26, 1649; Debien, "La question des Etats Généraux de 1649 et de 1651", *B. S. A. O.*, X, 598-620.

[84] *Ibid.*, pp. 620-38; Mss. de la Bibliothèque de Poitiers, 304 (42); Régistres de Poitiers, reg. 102, June 29, and July 3, 1651; A. D. Vienne, G 411, July 3, 1651.

[85] B. N., ms. fr. 4,184, fols. 366-76.

APPENDIX B

DOCUMENTS

1. *Vidimus*, dated May 19, 1402, of a letter of Charles VI, dated April 27, 1402, describing a grant made to him by an assembly of the clergy of Poitou. (B.N. ms. fr. 20,886, fol. 108).

   Comme les evesques de Poictiers Maillezois et Luçon les Abbez et autres gens deglise du pays de Poictou assemblez en la ville de Saint-Maixent pour ceste cause nous aient par vertu de certains privileges speciales a nous donne . . . ottroie gracieusement les aides ordonnez pour le fait de laguerre a nous estre paier en la somme et maniere acoustumee par le clerge et gens deglise dudit pays de Poictou jusques au terme de trois ans a en commencer le premier jour doctobre derienement passe tout ainsi que les prelats du royaume a Paris assemblez les nous octroient par semblable terme.

2. Account of the expenses incurred by the deputies from Poitiers in attending a meeting of the three estates of Poitou at Thouars, November 17-22, 1416. (A C. Poitiers, J. 547).

   Despence faicte par Perrotin Collet, commis ad ce par messeigneurs les mayre et commun de la ville de Poictiers a honorables hommes et saiges sire Jehan Larcher bourgoys d'icelle et a leurs varletz et chevaulx tant en alant de Poictiers a Thouars que pour leur retour a Poictiers lesquieulx furent commis de par ladicte ville pour aler audit lieu de Thouars obeir et comparoir par davant mons le viconte de Thouars mons. l'evesque de Clermont, maistre Guillaume Toreau et maistre Jehan de Luche commissaires ou pais de Poitou pour mons. le daulphin de Viennoys duc de Berri, conte de Pontieux et de Poitou sur le fait du gouvernement d'icelluy pays. Auquel lieu de Thouars mesdiz seigneurs avoient fait une convocation et assemblees des gens des trois estaz dudit pays de Poitou pour le fait, traitie et accort de mons. de Parthenay, ainsi qu'il appert plus a plain par les lettres desdiz mayre et commun donnees en plain mois et cent tenu le XVIe jour du moys d'octobre derrer passe par vertu desquelles lettres ledit Perrotin Collet a fait ladicte despense, ouquel veage mondit seigneur le mayre Jehan Larchier et Perrotin demourerent huyt jours tant en alant demourant que retornant a Poictiers pour ledit fait. C'est assavoir depuis le lundi XVIe jour du mois de novembre derrer passe jusques a l'autre lundi ensuivant XXIIIe jour d'icellui mois.

Premierement

Ledit lundi XVIe jour dudit mois de novembre mil CCCCXVI ou ilz partirent de Poitiers et a coucher a Mirebeau ... [a detailed account of day by day expenses follows.]

3. Letter of November 4, 1434 by Jean de la Roche, seneschal of Poitou, acknowledges receipt of 4000 *livres tournois* granted him by the estates of Poitou at a joint assembly held at Tours in August, 1434 with the estates of several other provinces. (B. N., Collection Clairambault, 194, fol. 7689).
[Jean de la Roche, seneschal of Poitou, acknowledges receipt of 4000 *livres* from Anthoine Vousy]
commis a recevoir oud. pais de poictou la porcion de laide octroie au Roy nostre Sire a lassemblee des trois estaz faicte en la ville de tours au mois daoust der. passe. [This sum of 4000 lt.] les gens des trois estaz dud. pais estans alad. assemblee ont consenti et accorde estre mise oudit pais oultre et pardessus le principal dud. aide cestasavoir 11m lt. pour partie de la somme de 1111m lt. a moy promise et accorde par lesd. gens des trois estaz dud. pais et aussi du pais de Xainctonge pour mectre le sige devant la ville daubeterre lors detenue et occuppee par les anglois Et les autres 11m lt. pour partie dautres 1111m lt. a moy semblablement promis et accorde par lesd. gens des trois estaz dudit pais de Poictou pour icelui pais garder et faire cesser en icelui les pilleries et aussi pour le delivrer des escossoys et autres gens deguerre de la compaignie de Symonnet de la tousche et pour autres causes plus a plain contenues ... es lettres patentes du Roy ... donnees a tours le deuxieme jour de septembre aussi derenierement passe.

4. Letter, dated June 1, 1447 by which three royal commissioners appoint a receiver to collect the sum of 18,000 *livres tournois* which the three estates of Poitou had granted the king in order to

be freed from the investigation of a royal commissioner whom he had sent to the province to investigate crimes and misdemeanors committed by various royal officials. (B. N., ms. fr. 20,887, fol. 1).
Guillaume evesque de Poictiers, Jehan Rabateau president en parlement et Jehan Bureau Tresorier de France Conseillers du Roy ntr Seigneur et ses commissaires en ceste partie a Jehan Bastier salut. Comme le Roy nostred. seigneur a la requeste des gens des trois estaz de ses pais et conte de poictou ait donne ses lettres dabolicion generales aux manans et habitans esd. pais et conte de poictou de tous les cas crimes deliz exces et malefices par eulz faiz et commis le temps passe dont mencion est faicte esdictes lettres dabolicion moiennant la somme de XVIIIm l.t. quilz ont pour ceste cause octroye aud. seigneur pour laquelle mectre sus imposer et egaler sur ceulx qui ont delinque et qui se vouldront aider de ladicte abolicion et estre comprins soubz icelle led. sire nous ait commis et ordonne par ses lettres patentes donnees a bourges ou moys de may dierement passe et par icelles nous ait donne povoir de commectre personne soufise et solvable a cueillir lever recevoir et faire venir ens lesdiz deniers et pour en rendre compte et Reliqua ou et quant il appartiendra. Savoir faisons que nous confions a plain de vos sens loyaute souffise et bonne diligence par vertu de nostrdit povoir vous avons commis et ordonne commectons et ordonnons par ces presentes a cueillir lever Recevoir amasser et faire venir ens iceulz deniers et pour les distribuer ou il vous sera ordonne par descharge du tresor et pour contraindre tous ceulx qui pour ce seront a contraindre et qui vous seront baillez par escript par nous ou nosdiz commis et deputez en ceste partie et qui vouldront estre comprins soubz ladicte abolicion et paier les sommes a quoy ilz avoient compose et este tauxez et imposez par nous ou nosdiz commis et deputez pour estre compris en ladicte abolicion par toutes voyes et manieres deues et raisonables et ainsi quil est acoustume de faire pour les propres debtes du Roy nostrdit sire Non obstant opposition ou appellacion quelconques pour lesquelles ne voulons inceulz deniers estre retardez. Si donnons en mandement par ces presentes de par le Roy nostredit Sire et nous a tous les justiciers officiers et subgiez dicellui Sire que a vous vos commis et depputez en ceste partie obeissent entendent diligemment et vous prestent et donnent conseil confort aide et prisons si mestier est et par vous ou vosdiz commis Requis en sont. Donne soubz noz sceaulx le premier jour de Juing lan mil CCCC quarante et sept.

5. Letter of 1484 (exact date blank in manuscript) by which Guil-
    laume d'Appelvoisin, sire de Pigny, acknowledges receipt of three
    hundred *livres tournois* for having attended the Estates General of
    Tours on behalf of the estates of Poitou. (A. N., KK 648, fol. 92,
    no. 85).

Je Guillaume dappelvoisin seigneur de Pigny confesse avoir eu et
receu de maistre Pierre Fauchet notaire et secretaire du Roy nostre
sire et Jehan Petit Receveur des tailles et paiement des gens de
guerre ou pais et comte de poictou la somme de troys cens livres
tourn. qui mont este tauxees par le Roy nostredit sire pour avoir
este et assiste pour les estatz du pais de poictou aux estatz generaulx
tenuz derrement a tours comme appert par les lectres patentes du
Roy nostredit sire de laquelle somme de trois cens livres tourn. je
me tiens pour content et bien paye et en ay quicte le Roy nostredit
sire lesd. Receveurs et tous autres. En tesmoigne de ce jay signe ces
presentes de mon seign manuel et scelle de mes armes. Le [blank
in manuscript] jour de [blank] lan mil CCCC 1111xx et quatre.

BIBLIOGRAPHY

UNPUBLISHED SOURCES

Of the documents preserved in the various archives and libraries of Paris, by far the most valuable for this work are to be found in the Bibliothèque Nationale, especially in the *manuscrits français* and the *pièces originales*. The Archives Nationales, although less useful, contains a number of valuable documents, most of which were in the series K and KK.

Town and departmental archives in Poitiers provided even more information. In fact, the most useful single depository of all was the Archives communales de Poitiers. Series C, H, I, J, K, and M contained considerable information, but the section of the town archives entitled Régistres des déliberations de la ville de Poitiers proved to be invaluable. It consists of the records of the deliberations of the town council, beginning in the year 1411. Unfortunately, there are gaps from July 27, 1461 to January 2, 1464, from March 1, 1482 to December 6, 1501, from July 11, 1524 to July 31, 1531, and from July 28, 1560 to July 1561. For the remainder of the period under study, however, these registers of deliberations provided invaluable information about the estates of Poitou. The communal archives of other towns in the area contained little of value.

The only part of the Archives départementales de la Vienne that contained any useful documents was series G concerning the secular clergy. This series threw considerable light upon the activities of the first estate at meetings of the three estates of Poitou during the sixteenth and seventeenth centuries. It was of no help for the earlier period. Of the other departmental archives of the region, the Archives départementales des Deux-Sèvres contained only two useful documents while the Archives de la Vendée contained nothing on the estates of Poitou.

One other collection of documents that bears mentioning is the Collection de Dom Fonteneau, preserved in the town library of Poitiers. This collection was gathered by Dom Fonteneau in the eighteenth century as the first step in the writing of a mammoth history of Aquitaine, a task which he never completed. It contains several documents concerning assemblies of the estates of Poitou in the sixteenth and seventeenth centuries.

In conclusion, it should be noted that most of the above sources were rather fragmentary and that they were extremely scattered. It was necessary to look through dozens of documents which yielded nothing for every one which proved useful. Nevertheless, by piecing together the many fragments which emerged, it was possible to gain a reasonably clear picture of the activities of the three estates of Poitou.

Archives communales de Poitiers

Series C, Gouvernement politique.
Documents concerning the estates of Poitou and the salt tax, 1549-1553.
– C 30, C 31, C 33.
Series G, Apétissement du dixième du vin vendu au détail.
Assembly of the estates of Poitou, January 1446. – G 19.
Series H, Barrages, octrois, et dons royaux.
Documents concerning assemblies of the estates of Poitou in 1393 and 1429.
– H 10, H 25.
Series I, Charges imposées par le souverain.
Documents concerning assemblies and taxes in Poitou in the fourteenth century. – I 1, I 3, I 6.
Series J, Charges communales.
Documents concerning assemblies of the estates of Poitou 1417-1461. – J 546,
J 547, J 553, J 554, J 644, J 735, J 905, J 906, J 1117, J 1118, J 1206, J 1207,
J 1210, J 1211, J 1277, J 1279.
Series K, Comptes de recette et de dépenses.
Documents concerning assemblies of the estates of Poitou in 1411 and 1461.
– K 4, K 7.
Series M, Recueils, inventaires, régistres divers.
The documents in register 11 concern meetings of the estates of Poitou between 1454 and 1529; those in register 15 concern the assembly of 1588. –
Régistre 11, fols. 1, 34, 59, and 62; régistre 15, fols. 68 and 69.

Régistres des déliberations

These registers are arranged in chronological order. Registers 1-6 contain documents describing meetings of the estates of Poitou during the reigns of Charles VI, Charles VII, and Louis XI. Registers 30-32 contain documents describing the assemblies of 1549-53 regarding salt taxes. Registers 42, 48, 69, 100, 102 and 103 contain information about meetings of the estates of Poitou held to elect deputies to the Estates General during the period 1576-1651. – Régistres 1, 2, 3, 4, 6, 30, 31, 32, 42, 48, 69, 100, 102, and 103.

An inventory for the Archives communales de Poitiers is published in *Mémoires de la Société des Antiquaires de l'Ouest,* series 2, V (1882). It does not include the Régistres des déliberations.

Archives départementales de la Vienne

Series G, Secular clergy.
Documents on assemblies of the clergy of Poitou between 1560 and 1651. –
G 395, G 398-403, G 411, G 1310.

Archives départementales des Deux-Sèvres

Series C.
Financial documents regarding taxes and possible assemblies in Poitou in 1529 and 1350 respectively. – C 12 and C 17.

Archives historiques de la ville de Fontenay-le-Comte, réunis et mises en ordre par Benjamin Fillon avec la collaboration d'A. Bitton, II, 185, and III, 269-72

These are nineteenth century copies of original documents concerning assemblies of the estates of Poitou in 1549 and 1614.

Archives Nationales

Series K, Monuments historiques.
Documents concerning taxes imposed by Charles VII in Poitou. – K 63, nos. 25 and 36; K 64, no. 11; K 67, no. 10.
Series KK, Régistres.
Documents concerning taxes and assemblies of estates in Poitou, 1393-1483. – KK 337; KK 346; KK 648, fols. 91 and 92.
Series P, Chambre des Comptes.
Document concerning the ratification of the Treaty of Etaples by various particular estates, including those of Poitou. – P 2302, pp. 789-92.
Series X, Parlement de Paris.
Legal cases arising from assemblies of the estates of Poitou in c. 1382 and c. 1451-54. – X^{1c}46B, no. 207; X^{2a}41.

Bibliothèque municipale de Poitiers

This collection has been renumbered. The number in brackets indicates the older classification. These two documents concern the estates of Poitou in 1651 and 1549 respectively. – Mss. 304 (42); 384 (36), pp. 355-56.
Collection de Dom Fonteneau.
This collection is preserved in the municipal library of Poitiers. These documents concern assemblies of the estates of Poitou between 1549 and 1614. – II, 425, 428, and 447; XII, 469; XIV, 739; XXIII, 185; XXVII, ter., 141; XL, 54; LX, 457; LXXIV, 331-74.

Bibliothèque Nationale

Manuscrits français.
Miscellaneous documents relative to the estates of Poitou, 1390-1651. The largest number are from the reigns of Charles VI, Charles VII, and Louis XI, and are financial in nature. – 3086, fols. 98 and 110; 3901, fol. 57; 3910, fol. 111; 4184, fol. 371; 4189, fol. 257; 5497; 5501, fol. 82; 6199, no. 3; 6200; 6741; 6742; 6747, fols. 1 and 20; 12,041; 15,637; 15,871, p. 87; 16,257; 20,084, pp. 43, 46, and 57; 20,157, fol. 153; 20,583, fol. 52; 20,594, nos. 25 and 27; 20,685, pp. 408, 435, and 494; 20,886, fols. 108, 109, 110, 113 and 114; 20,887, fol. 1; 21,423, fols. 23, 26, 34, 74, 103, and 132; 21,428, fol. 9; 22,731, fols. 23 and 24; 23,291; 23,292; 23,909, fols. 1 and 5; 23,935, fol. 212; 25,969, no. 956; 26,073, no. 5172; 32,511, fols. 100, 102, 113, 115, 124, 277, 283, and 318; n.a., 1118; n.a., 3624, no. 369; n.a., 3638; n.a., 3654; n.a., 5233, no. 10; n.a., 7853; n.a., 10,018.

Collection Clairambault.
    Most of these documents concern meetings of the estates of Poitou between
    the years 1418 and 1434. – 23, p. 1641; 58, p. 4427; 105, p. 8223; 193, fol.
    7563, no. 14; 194, fols. 7689 and 7691; 354, p. 5385.
Collection Dupuy.
    Assemblies within the *gouvernement* of Orleans in June 1561 to elect deputies
    to the Estates General. – 588, fols. 45, 47, and 57.
Collection de Périgord.
    Documents concerning the regional assemblies of 1549. – XXIV, fols. 336
    and 343.
Collection des Cinq Cents de Colbert.
    Description of assemblies within the *gouvernement* of Guyenne in March
    1561 to elect deputies to the Estates General. – 27, fols. 303 and 325.
Pièces originales.
    The pièces originales consist of documents concerning various notable fami-
    lies. Those listed below are all from the fifteenth century. The majority are
    acknowledgements by various individuals of sums of money granted them by
    the estates of Poitou. – Vol. 47, Amboise, no. 59; vol. 89, Argenton; vol.
    201, La Barre, no. 9; vol. 247, Beaumont, doss. 5423, nos. 2 and 3; vol. 365,
    Blandin, doss. 7912, nos. 3, 4, 5, 6, and 7; vol. 368, de Blet, doss. 8023,
    no. 2; vol. 450, Boulligny, doss. 10,158, no. 15; vol. 772, Claveurier, doss.
    17,625, nos. 2 and 15; vol. 1324, Gilier, doss. 29,964, no. 22; vol. 1612,
    Labbé, doss. 37,421, nos. 3 and 4; vol. 1849, Mareuil, doss. 42,690, pp. 24
    and 31; vol. 2374, Précigny, doss. 53,271, no. 12; vol. 2404, du Puy du Fou,
    doss. 53,880, no. 14; vol. 2855, Torsay, doss. 63,456, nos. 11, 13, and 14;
    vol. 2896, Le Tur, doss. 64,363, no. 11; vol. 3041, Vousy, doss. 67,419, nos.
    3 and 6.

PUBLISHED SOURCES

Archives Communales d'Amboise, AA 144, pub. Abbé C. Chevalier, *Inventaire
    analytique des archives communales d'Amboise* (Tours, Georget-Joubert,
    1874).
Archives historiques du département de la Gironde, vol. XXVIII (1893), 49.
    This document describes an assembly at Poitiers in 1550 at which deputies
    from Poitou and Guyenne were present.
Archives historiques du Poitou, vols. II (1873), XI (1881), XIII (1883), XIV (1883),
    XV (1883), XIX (1888), XX (1889), XXVI (1896), XXVII (1896), XXIX
    (1898), XXXI (1901), XXXVI (1907), XLIV (1923), XLVI (1928), and
    XLVIII (1934).
    The most valuable collection of published documents for the history of the
    region. Volumes XI, XIII, XIX, XXVI, and XXIX consist of a collection of
    documents compiled by Paul Guérin concerning Poitou, taken from the
    registers of the French chancery during the period 1302-1430. Volumes XIV,
    XV, XXVII, and XXXVI contain memoirs, letters, and journals concerning
    Poitou during the sixteenth and seventeenth centuries. Volumes XLIV and
    XLVI are collections of documents compiled by Edouard Audouin concern-
    ing the town of Poitiers during the period 1063-1380. The other volumes
    cited above contain miscellaneous documents concerning the estates of Poitou
    during the fifteenth and sixteenth centuries.

Bouchet, Jean, *Les Annales d'Aquitaine* (Poitiers, A. Mounin, 1644).
Written by a sixteenth century Poitevin historian who participated personally in the dispute over the salt taxes, 1549-1553.

Bourdot de Richebourg, C. A., *Nouveau Coutumier général*, vol. IV (Paris, M. Brunet, 1724).
The most valuable source of information about assemblies for the codification of the customs of Poitou.

Charrier, G., ed., *Les Jurades de la ville de Bergerac*, vols. I and III (Bergerac, Imprimerie générale du Sud-Ouest, 1892).

D'Aussy, D., ed., *Régistres de l'échevinage de Saint-Jean d'Angély, Archives de la ville de Saint-Jean d'Angély*, CCXIX, *Archives Historiques de la Saintonge et de l'Aunis*, XXXII (1902).

Documents inédits pour servir à l'histoire du Poitou, publiés par la Société des Antiquaires de l'Ouest (Poitiers, 1876), pp. 157-58.
Describes an assembly of the estates of Poitou on July 11, 1549.

Fillon, B., ed., *Documents pour servir à l'histoire du Bas-Poitou,* Vol. I (Fontenay-le-Comte, 1847).

Froissart, Jean, *Chroniques*, Vol. VII, ed. Siméon Luce, *Société de l'Histoire de France*, 1878.

La Boutetière, L. de, ed., "Rôle des tailles en Poitou au XVe siècle", *Mémoires de la Société des Antiquaires de l'Ouest*, series 2, II (1878-79), 499.

La Fontenelle de Vaudoré, Armand de, ed., *Journal de Guillaume et Michel le Riche, avocats du roi à Saint-Maixent de 1534 à 1586* (Saint-Maixent, Reversé, 1846).
Only useful for the assembly of 1576.

La Trémoïlle, Louis de, ed., *Livre de comptes de Guy de la Trémoïlle (1395-1406)* (Nantes, Forest et Grimaud, 1887).

Laurière, Secousse, et al., eds., *Ordonnances des rois de France de la troisième race*, XX (Paris, Imprimerie Royale, 1723-1849).

Masselin, Jean, *Journal des Etats Généraux tenus à Tours en 1484 sous le règne de Charles VIII*, ed. A. Bernier, *Collection des documents inédits sur l'histoire de France*, 1835.

Mayer, Charles, *Des Etats Généraux et autres assemblées nationales*, vols. VII, XIII, and XIV (La Haye, et se trouve à Paris chez Buisson, 1788-89).

Molinier, A., ed., *Correspondence administrative d'Alphonse de Poitiers*, 2 vols., *Collection de documents inédits sur l'histoire de France* (Paris, Imprimerie Nationale, 1894-1900).

Ordonnances des rois de France, règne de François Ier. Académie des Sciences Morales et Politiques, vol. VI, part 1 (Paris, 1902-42).

Pélicier, P., ed., *Lettres de Charles VIII, Roi de France*, vol. V. *Société de l'Histoire de France* (1905).

Quinet, Toussaint, *Recueil général des estats tenus en France sous les rois Charles VI, Charles VIII, Charles IX, Henri III, et Louis XIII* (Paris, Publisher unknown, 1651).

Richard, Alfred, ed., *Inventaire-Sommaire des archives communales antérieures à 1790 de Saint-Maixent* (Paris, Paul Dupont, 1863).

Rymer, Thomas, *Foedera, conventiones, litterae, et cujuscunque generis acta publica*, vol. V, part 2 (Hagae Comitis, Apud Joannem Neaulme, 1741), pp. 89-91.
Describes the assembly of the estates of Poitou of March 28, 1497 for the ratification of the Treaty of Etaples.

Teilhard de Chardin, E., ed., "Régistres de Barthélemi de Noces, officier du Duc de Berry (1374-1377)", *Bibliothèque de l'Ecole des Chartes*, LII (1891), 220-58 and 517-72.
Vaësen, J., and Charavay, E., eds., *Lettres de Louis XI*, vol. X. *Société de l'Histoire de France* (1908).

BOOKS

Beaucourt, G. du Fresne de, *Histoire de Charles VII*, 6 vols. (Paris, Alphonse Picard, 1881-1891).
Bisson, Thomas, *Assemblies And Representation In Languedoc In The Thirteenth Century* (Princeton, Princeton University Press, 1964).
Boutaric, Edgar, *Saint Louis et Alphonse de Poitiers* (Paris, Henri Plon, 1870).
Callery, Alphonse, *Histoire de l'origine, des pouvoirs, et des attributions des états généraux et provinciaux depuis la féodalité jusqu'aux états de 1355* (Brussels, Alfred Vromant, 1881).
Cosneau, E., *Le Connétable de Richemont* (Paris, Hachette, 1886).
Delachenal, R., *Histoire de Charles V*, 5 vols. (Paris, Alphonse Picard, 1909-1931).
Delcambre, Etienne, *Les Etats du Velay des origines à 1642* (Le Puy, L'auteur, 1938).
Doucet, Roger, *Les Institutions de la France au XVIe siècle*, 2 vols. (Paris, A. and J. Picard, 1948).
Dupont-Ferrier, Gustave, *Essai sur la géographie administrative des élections financières en France de 1356 à 1790. Annuaire-Bulletin de la Société de l'Histoire de France.* LXV and LXVI (1928-1929).
——, *Gallia Regia, ou état des officiers royaux des baillages et sénéchaussées de 1328 à 1515*, 4 vols. (Paris, Imprimerie Nationale, 1942-1954).
——, *Les officiers royaux des baillages et sénéchaussées à la fin du moyen âge* (Paris, Librarie Emile Bouillon, 1902).
Favre, L., *Histoire de la ville de Niort depuis son origine jusqu'en 1789* (Niort, Favre, 1880).
Filhol, René, *Le premier président Christofle de Thou et la réformation des coutumes* (Paris, Librairie du Recueil Sirey, 1937).
——, *Le vieux coustumier de Poictou* (Bourges, Editions Tardy, 1956).
Gilles, Henri, *Les Etats de Languedoc au XVe siècle*, in *Bibliothèque Méridionale*, Second Series, no. 40 (Toulouse, Edouard Privat, 1965). —
Girard, Joseph, *Les Etats du Comté Venaissin depuis leurs origines jusqu'à la fin du XVIe siècle* (Paris, H. Champion, 1908).
Hanotaux, Gabriel, *Histoire du Cardinal de Richelieu*, vol. I (Paris, Firmin-Didot, 1896).
Hirschauer, Charles, *Les Etats d'Artois de leurs origines à l'occupation française, 1340-1640*, 2 vols. (Paris, H. Champion – Brussels, Henri Lamertin, 1923).
Imbert, Hugues, *Histoire de Thouars* (Niort, Clouzot, 1871).
Lacour, René, *Le Gouvernement de l'apanage de Jean, Duc de Berry, 1360-1416* (Paris, Editions Auguste Picard, 1934).
Laferrière, F., *Etude sur l'histoire et l'organisation comparée des états provinciaux aux diverses époques de la monarchie jusqu'en 1789. Séances et Travaux de l'Académie des Sciences Morales et Politiques*, LIII-LIX (1860-1862).
La Trémoïlle, Louis, Duc de, *Les La Trémoïlle pendant cinq siècles*, 5 vols. (Nantes, E. Grimaud, 1890-1896).

Ledain, Bélisaire, *La Gâtine historique et monumentale* (Paris, Imprimerie Claye, 1876).

——, *Histoire de la ville de Parthenay, de des anciens seigneurs, et de la Gâtine du Poitou* (Poitiers, A. Durand, 1858).

——, *Histoire sommaire de la ville de Poitiers* (Fontenay-le-Comte, Baud, 1889).

Lot, Ferdinand, and Fawtier, Robert, *Histoire des institutions françaises au moyen âge*, vol. I (Paris, Presses Universitaires de France, 1957).

Lousse, Emile, *La Société de l'Ancien Régime*, I. *Etudes présentées à la Commission Internationale pour l'Histoire des Assemblées d'Etats*, VI, in *Recueil de Travaux d'Histoire et de Philologie* (Université de Louvain), series 3, no. 16 (Louvain, Editions Universitas – Bruges, Desclee, de Brouwer et Cie, 1943).

Luchaire, Achille, *Manuel des institutions françaises* (Paris, Hachette, 1892).

Major, J. Russell, *The Deputies To The Estates General In Renaissance France* (Madison, University of Wisconsin Press, 1960).

Olivier-Martin, François, *Histoire du droit français des origines à la Révolution* (Paris, Editions Domat Montchrestien, 1951).

Picot, Georges, *Histoire des Etats Généraux*, 4 vols. (Paris, Hachette, 1872).

Prentout, Henri, *Les Etats provinciaux de Normandie*, in *Mémoires de l'Académie Nationale des Sciences, Arts, et Belles-Lettres de Caen*, Nouvelle série, vols. I and II (Caen, Imprimerie E. Lanier, 1925).

Rébillon, A., *Les Etats de Bretagne de 1661 à 1789* (Paris, Editions Auguste Picard – Rennes, Plihon, 1932).

Sée, Henri, *Louis XI et les villes* (Paris, Hachette, 1891).

Strayer, Joseph A., and Taylor, Charles H., *Studies In Early French Taxation* (Cambridge, Mass., Harvard University Press, 1939).

Thibaudeau, Antoine, *Histoire du Poitou*, 3 vols. (Niort, Robin, 1839-1840).

Thomas, Antoine, *Les Etats provinciaux de la France centrale sous Charles VII* (Paris, Champion, 1879).

Vallet de Viriville, M., *Mémoire sur les institutions de Charles VII* (Paris, Librairie Renouard, 1872).

Viollet, Paul, *Droit publique: histoire des institutions politiques et administratives de la France*, 3 vols. (Paris, L. Larose et Forcel, 1890-1903).

ARTICLES

Babeau, Albert, "La représentation du Tiers Etat aux assemblées pour la rédaction des coutumes au XVIe siècle", *Revue Historique*, XXI (1883), 91-100.

Callery, A., "Les états provinciaux sous Charles VII", *Revue des Questions Historiques*, XXVII (1880), 584-92.

——, "L'origine des Etats Généraux et provinciaux", *Annales de la Faculté des Lettres de Bordeaux* (1882), 127-38.

Cam, Helen, Marongiu, Antonio, and Stökl, Gunther, "Recent Works and Present Views on the Origins and Development of Representative Assemblies", *X Congresso Internazionale Di Scienze Storiche, Relazioni I* (Firenze, 1955), 1-101.

Cardenal, L. de, "Catalogue des assemblées des Etats de Périgord de 1378 à 1651", *Bulletin Philologique et Historique du Comité des Travaux Historiques et Scientifiques* (1938-1939), 240-69.

D'Aussy, D., "La Saintonge pendant la Guerre de Cent Ans", *Bulletin de la Société des Archives Historiques de la Saintonge et de l'Aunis*, XIV (1894), 217-21, and 354-94.

Debien, G., "La question des Etats Généraux de 1649 et de 1651: la convocation et les élections en Haut-Poitou", *Bulletin de la Société des Antiquaires de l'Ouest*, series 3, X (1934-1935), 598-641.

Delcambre, E., "Les origines des Etats du Velay", *Etudes présentées à la Commission Internationale pour l'Histoire des Assemblées d'Etats*, III (1939), 157-62.

Déruelle, Commandant, "La révolte de la gabelle en Angoumois et en Saintonge (1548-1549)", *Bulletin de la Société des Archives Historiques. Revue de la Saintonge et de l'Aunis*, XXVII (1907), 91-102 and 170-84.

Dupont-Ferrier, G., "De quelques problèmes historiques relatifs aux états provinciaux", *Journal des Savants* (August-October, 1928), 315-57.

——, "Des problèmes relatifs aux états dits provinciaux", *Journal des Savants* (1939), 301-30.

——, "Les origines des élections financières en France aux XIVe et XVe siècles", *Bibliothèque de l'Ecole des Chartes*, XC (1929), 233-55.

Hanotaux, G., "La Jeunesse de Richelieu", *Revue des Deux Mondes*, XCIV (August, 1889), 566-605.

La Boutetière, L. de, "Un impôt de guerre en 1479", *Annuaire Départementale de la Société d'Emulation de la Vendée*, series 2, IX (1879), 68-91.

Lacroix, Abbé L., "Richelieu à Luçon – Sa jeunesse, son épiscopat", *Mémoires de la Société des Antiquaires de l'Ouest*, series 2, XII (1889), 79-109.

Ledain, B., "Les Maires de Poitiers". *Mémoires de la Société des Antiquaires de l'Ouest*, LX (1879), 215-398.

Lousse, E., "Assemblées d'Etats", *L'Organisation corporative du Moyen Age à la fin de l'Ancien Régime. Etudes présentées à la Commission Internationale pour l'Histoire des Assemblées d'Etats*, VII (Louvain, 1943), 233-63.

——, "La formation des ordres dans la société médiévale", *L'Organisation corporative du Moyen Age à la fin de l'Ancien Régime. Etudes présentées à la Commission Internationale pour l'Histoire des Assemblées d'Etats*, II (Louvain, 1937), 61-90.

Major, J. R., "The Electoral Procedure For The Estates General Of France And Its Social Implications, 1483-1651", *Medievalia et Humanistica*, X (1956), 131-50.

——, "The Payment Of The Deputies To The French National Assemblies, 1484-1627", *Journal of Modern History*, XXVII (1955), 217-29.

——, "The Third Estate In The Estates General of Pontoise, 1561", *Speculum*, XXIX (1954), 460-76.

Merle, Dr. L., "Un cahier de doléances d'une paroisse rurale pour les Etats Généraux de 1649: Saint-Christophe-sur-Roc", *Bulletin de la Société Historique et Scientifique des Deux-Sèvres*, IX (1951), 86-91.

Mirot, Léon, "Les Etats Généraux et provinciaux et l'abolition des aides au début du règne de Charles VI (1380-81)", *Revue des Questions Historiques*, LXXIV (1903), 398-455.

Molinier, A., "Etats provinciaux", *La Grande Encyclopédie*, XVI, 523-27.

Niel, Abbé L., "Histoire des évêques de Tulle. Hugues de Combarel, XIIIe évêque", *Bulletin de la Société des Lettres, Sciences, et Arts de la Corrèze*, X (1888), 52-97.

Ninglat, P., "Des états provinciaux sous le règne de Louis XIV", *Revue des Sociétés Savantes des Départements*, series 2, II (1859), 57-72.

Ouvré, H., "Essai sur l'histoire de la Ligue à Poitiers", *Mémoires de la Société des Antiquaires de l'Ouest*, series I, XXI (1854), 103-98.

Picot, G., "Le droit électoral de l'ancienne France. Les élections aux Etats Généraux dans les provinces de 1302 à 1614", *Extrait du Compte-Rendu de l'Académie des Sciences Morales et Politiques,* CII (July-December, 1874), 20-33, and 208-21.

Prentout, H., "Les états provinciaux en France", *Bulletin Of The International Committee Of Historical Sciences,* I (Washington, 1828), 632-34.

Ravan, H., "Etat des nobles du Poitou à l'occasion de l'aide extraordinaire offerte à F. de la Trémoïlle, commissaire général du roi en Poitou et Saintonge pour le rachat de la rançon du roi François Ier après la bataille de Pavie", *Mémoires de la Société de Statistique du Département des Deux-Sèvres,* series 2, I (1860-1861), 51-81.

Richard, A., "Recherches sur l'organisation communale de la ville de Saint-Maixent jusqu'en 1790", *Mémoires de la Société des Antiquaires de l'Ouest,* series 1, XXXIV (1869), 324-79.

Taylor, C. H., "The Composition Of Baronial Assemblies In France, 1315-1320", *Speculum,* XXIX (1954), 433-59.

Thomas, A., "Les Etats Généraux sous Charles VII", *Revue Historique,* XL (1889), 55-88.

——, "Nouveaux documents sur les états provinciaux de la Haute Marche (1418-1446)", *Annales du Midi,* XXV (1913), 429-52.

Viard, Jules, "Les ressources extraordinaires de la royauté sous Philippe VI de Valois", *Revue des Questions Historiques,* XLIV (1888), 167-218.

Vuitry, A., "L'origine et l'établissement de l'impôt sous les trois premiers Valois (1328-1380)", *Compte-Rendu de l'Académie des Sciences Morales et Politiques,* XIX (1883), 696-720, and 868-88, XX (1884), 68-91.

UNPUBLISHED THESES

Berranger, Henri de, "La sénéchaussée de Poitou de la mort d'Alphonse de Poitiers à l'occupation anglaise (1271-1361). Etude sur l'administration royale", Unpublished thesis for the Ecole des Chartes, 1924.
One of the two original handwritten copies of this thesis is preserved in the Archives départementales de la Vienne.

La Martinière, Jules Machet de, "Les guerres anglaises dans l'ouest et le centre de la France (1403-1417)", Unpublished thesis for the Ecole des Chartes, 1899.
The brief *position de thèse* is preserved in the Archives départementales de la Vienne, F 22. The thesis itself is not available.

INDEX

STUDIES IN EUROPEAN HISTORY

MOUTON · PUBLISHERS · THE HAGUE